Principal Presence, Principal Mystique

Principal Presence, Principal Mystique

Five Systems to Prioritize Your Time
and Implement Best Practices

Courtney Gober

BLOOMSBURY ACADEMIC
NEW YORK • LONDON • OXFORD • NEW DELHI • SYDNEY

BLOOMSBURY ACADEMIC
Bloomsbury Publishing Inc, 1359 Broadway, New York, NY 10018, USA
Bloomsbury Publishing Plc, 50 Bedford Square, London, WC1B 3DP, UK
Bloomsbury Publishing Ireland, 29 Earlsfort Terrace, Dublin 2, D02 AY28, Ireland

BLOOMSBURY, BLOOMSBURY ACADEMIC and the Diana logo are trademarks of
Bloomsbury Publishing Plc

First published in the United States of America 2026

Bloomsbury Publishing Inc does not have any control over, or responsibility for, any third-
party websites referred to or in this book. All internet addresses given in this book were
correct at the time of going to press. The author and publisher regret any inconvenience
caused if addresses have changed or sites have ceased to exist, but can accept no
responsibility for any such changes.

A catalog record for this book is available from the Library of Congress

ISBN: HB: 979-8-2163-7626-2
Pbk: 979-8-2163-7625-5
ePDF: 979-8-2163-7628-6
eBook: 979-8-2163-7627-9

Typeset by Deanta Global Publishing Services, Chennai, India
Printed and bound in the United States of America

For product safety related questions contact productsafety@bloomsbury.com.

To find out more about our authors and books visit www.bloomsbury.com and
sign up for our newsletters.

To the remarkable staff and students I've had the honor of working alongside throughout my career. To the assistant principals who have been more than colleagues—true partners in the pursuit of educational excellence—thank you for your collaboration and commitment.

My deepest gratitude goes to Dr. Billy Pringle, Executive Director of TASSP. Your steadfast support and encouragement were instrumental in bringing this book to life. I am truly grateful for your belief in me.

Special thanks to the extraordinary mentors and principal role models who have shaped my leadership journey: Sara Bonser, Kathy King, Dr. Tom Maglisceau, Burt Smith, and Laurie Taylor. Your influence and example continue to guide me.

Most importantly, to my family—especially my children— thank you for being my foundation and inspiration. Your love, patience, and unwavering support have been my greatest source of strength.

Contents

Part II How We Do School <inline>47</inline>

Part III The Predictable Principal

—

Introduction

The idea of writing a book that truly contributes to our profession and, more importantly, helps principals is absolutely daunting but is also my absolute intent. I want to help principals navigate best practices and tame their time to focus on instructional leadership. This book is not full of new ideas; it is full of best practices and real-life examples of how to best implement them.

Are there even any new ideas to write about? In 2012, Peter DeWitt, a former elementary principal and renowned school leadership coach and author, wrote a short article for *Education Week* titled: "Todd Whitaker Already Said It." DeWitt recalled a conversation with his editor that led to this article about Todd Whitaker, a former principal and author of over sixty books who is considered an authority on school leadership.

> [He] contacted me because he saw an article I wrote that he liked and wondered if I ever considered writing a book. He thought I had potential, and everyone who writes understands that the conversation around a book is only one small step. As honored as I was, and as hard as I tried, I did not have any original ideas. I simply wrote him back and said I was sorry but anything I would want to write has been written by Todd Whitaker already.

To even think that I would have anything to contribute to this topic is preposterous. Even if DeWitt was wrong, I am sure that any unclaimed pearls of wisdom have been shared over the last decade. I am not a DeWitt or Whitaker—I am just a former principal who learned how to silence the noise of administrivia so that I could maintain a calendar that reflected my priorities and implement the systems that yielded the best student outcomes.

There is no how-to book, step-by-step manual, or turnkey approach to being a principal. For clarity, there should not be such a tool. After all, being a principal is being a dynamic, instructional leader who has gained the experiences of school leadership by serving as a teacher and assistant principal for enough time to understand the workings of a school and how to positively move the instructional needle.

In 1999, the Wallace Foundation commissioned a comprehensive study on school leadership. The study, published in 2004 and called "How Leadership Influences Student Learning," explored how school leadership directly and indirectly influences student learning and overall school improvement. One question they sought to answer was whether principals have an impact on student learning. The findings of this study revealed that school leadership was second only to teaching among indicators that affect student learning (Leithwood et al., 2004). It was a game changer in the field of educational leadership.

The Wallace Foundation's work in this area continued to evolve, with ongoing research and initiatives aimed at strengthening school leadership nationwide. Twenty years later, they commissioned a new study that resulted in the 2021 publication *How Principals Affect Students and Schools: A Systemic Synthesis of Two Decades of Research* (Grissom et al., 2021). This research synthesized hundreds of studies to better understand the behaviors principals exhibit to produce positive school outcomes. It concluded that effective principals carry out four key practices:

- Focus on instruction in their interactions with teachers
- Build a productive school climate
- Promote collaboration and professional learning among teachers and others
- Manage personnel and resources well

This study empowered me to share systems and practices that worked for my schools. In the last decade, I found myself leaving the principal's chair and moving to the district office to work with principals both as their supervisor and as a district support. When I examined these four key practices against what I was trying to do as a principal and how I was coaching as a principal supervisor, I realized I was on the right track. Yes, I needed to modify here and there. I certainly needed to enhance my focus on instruction when interacting with teachers. However, I had met, and nearly perfected, the challenge of fitting everything considered necessary for effective school leadership into a principal's unquestionably hectic schedule.

I have had countless conversations with new principals about their preparation and readiness for the principalship. I have observed what happens to most new principals when they start their new positions: they do what has always been done at their campus with minor, even token, adjustments and follow the close direction of the district office. Of course! This is expected. No one wants to start their principal career by making waves and possibly ending their career early. It is difficult for a new principal to discern what systems to implement and how to monitor them.

Research has continually revealed that "Principals really matter. Indeed, it is difficult to envision an investment with a higher ceiling on its potential return than a successful effort to improve principal leadership" (Grissom et al., 2021, p. xiv). *Principal Presence, Principal Mystique* is meant to motivate all school principals to reach the full measure of their impact and influence on student achievement at their school. It should serve as a catalyst to inspect your systems and hit the reset button where needed to lead and manage your school. It provides an outline of how to enhance your **Principal Presence** and **Principal Mystique** while maintaining a calendar that reflects the priorities and high expectations you have for yourself and your school.

Principal Presence, Principal Mystique

The underlying strategies I use are **Principal Presence** and **Principal Mystique**. **Principal Presence** is the subtle revelation of the influence I bear as principal. From establishing the mission and vision for the campus to setting goals and expectations, all stakeholders either see or feel my influence and involvement in shaping a positive school culture focused on student achievement. Remember, both the 2004 and 2021 Wallace studies overwhelmingly proved that principals really matter! The act of monitoring, engaging, and participating in five systems vital for school success means that I do not merely implement levers for school improvement; I control them via **Principal Presence**. It may initially sound like I am a micromanager or am power hungry, but as you continue through this book, you will see how **Principal Presence** is unveiled and utilized in a positive, productive manner that empowers and builds efficacy for your staff and students.

The other strategy I employ is **Principal Mystique**. This entails feeding the belief that on this campus, "I am everywhere" and "I know about everything that happens." Throughout the book, I explain how I constantly feed the belief that I am on top of things and always "in the know" to students, staff, and parents. As you read, you will slowly be able to see the wizard behind the curtain.

The strategies **Principal Presence** and **Principal Mystique** are in bold throughout the book for two reasons: I want to ensure my readers see the connection between the strategy and the system, and I want the reader to imagine a ghost-like voice echoing in their mind, "Principal Presence and Principal Mystique," as these strategies are revealed.

Principals don't have auto-pilot. The systems and structures outlined here work interdependently and do not have a "cruise control" or "autonomous drive mode." These systems require regular monitoring and attention with the goal of creating a school that operates at a high level of efficiency and effectiveness.

The key to these systems, like anything, is to persist and make each one a priority in your leadership. You define your priorities with the energy, money, and TIME you dedicate. You cannot delegate **Principal Presence** or **Principal Mystique**—you can share but not delegate. Why? Principals really matter! Your attention, presence, and time matter! Due to my belief that time defines importance, this book, unlike many others, provides guidance on how to shape your calendar to implement these systems. It will all come together in Chapter 12, "Your Time," where you can exhale any anxiety and pressure that you may be experiencing.

This book addresses the key practices mentioned in the Wallace study by explaining how to implement five systems I have found to be manageable, practical, and palatable for all stakeholders. I also share structures to organize your school staff, tools, and practices for better communication. I'll show you how to prioritize your time by building a principal calendar that allows you to effectively maneuver the levers of school improvement and get closer to realizing the high reliability school that Marzano et al. (2014) and others have so eloquently described. Please note that, like anything, your persistence will bring about consistency, which in turn establishes predictability, routines, and a culture of high expectations. The goal is to use your **Principal Presence** and **Principal Mystique** to create a seamless set of systems that evolve into the understanding that "this is how we do school."

1 When I'm Principal

When I become principal, I will engage my students, support my teachers, and be visible to the community. I will move the needle and close learning gaps for all students. I know I am ready. I know I can do it. Someone just needs to give me a chance.
EVERY ASPIRING PRINCIPAL

The debate over whether great leaders are innately destined for greatness or shaped by their experiences and circumstances endures. This question often occupies my thoughts when reflecting on the making of exceptional school principals. It seems rather simplistic to assert that principals are born into greatness, yet one might argue that they were born with inherent leadership qualities, and fate guided them to the role of principal. Ultimately, I consistently arrive at the same conclusion: great principals are crafted and refined through their experiences, beginning with their foundations as exemplary teachers. In my view, the journey of a great principal follows a trajectory.

The Confident Teacher

The confidence you had as a classroom teacher was evident not only in the classroom but also in your team meetings, staff meetings, and campus and district committee work. A simple conversation with you about teaching would show anyone that you were a confident teacher. You understood your content and could predict the lessons and units that your students would struggle with. To overcome those struggles, you collected tried-and-true strategies that allowed your students to share this feeling of confidence—not just in you but also in themselves.

Teaching was frustrating and overwhelming when you first started. You had to learn all of the rules and laws around confidentiality, safety, security, and students with disabilities, as well as know about foods of minimal nutritional value, not to mention pedagogy and child development. Nevertheless, you navigated through those beginning years, being sure to check every box, dot every i, and cross every t, because the last thing you wanted was to break a rule or inadvertently underserve a child. Along the way, you learned more about instructional best practices, including how to differentiate lessons, assess learning, create interventions, and better engage your students. You subconsciously intertwined your natural personality and comfort level with all that you learned so that you could deliver high-quality instruction as measured by any assessment.

Assessment? Yes, you learned how to read and interpret the data from assessments to inform your instructional decision-making, especially for those students who were more dependent as learners. You created your own assessments, both formative and summative, and you procured a plethora of tools throughout your career that included successful strategies and interventions for the most common dilemmas you encountered as a teacher. You were a master teacher. You knew what to do, how to do it, and when to do it.

Over time, you were asked to serve on committees or write curriculum. Perhaps you were even given a leadership role on campus as a team leader or department chair. You understood that these new opportunities allowed you to expand the reach of your influence beyond your classroom, and you carefully began to develop a new set of skills as a leader. Always careful not to overstep your role, you worked collaboratively with teachers and leaders from both your campus and district to improve instruction for all students. You may have also found yourself serving as a mentor for newer, less confident teachers or even been fortunate enough to have a student teacher from the local university. You shared your best lessons and intervention strategies and created collaborative opportunities where everyone contributed and felt valued by your guidance.

Administrators and other colleagues hinted to you about becoming an administrator. You politely smiled outwardly and inwardly thought that you could probably do it, perhaps even better than the current administrators. You began to look into the requirements needed to become an administrator, talked with your family and friends, and decided to go for it.

Assistant Principal: From Firefighter to Lifeguard

After completing the necessary coursework and state credentials, you quickly got snatched up as an assistant principal (AP). Whoa, you felt your confidence level waning but decided not to dwell on it because you just needed time and experience to learn more rules and create more space in your existing toolbox for best practices and strategies that crossed content areas and grade levels.

Your years as an AP were an emotional roller coaster; most days, you felt like a firefighter constantly reacting to the emails, phone calls, discipline referrals, and calls on the walkie-talkie. You worked with some tough parents, students, and even teachers who allowed you to use the strategies and tools from your teaching years, only to discover that you still needed to learn more. You especially needed to become more comfortable and proficient with crucial conversations.

You tried to be everywhere at all times to solve all the problems and make a name for yourself as a supporter of teachers and advocate for all students. Some teachers became frequent flyers for your assistance, always willing to drop their problems on your doorstep and watch you work your magic. Some students became regular customers, too, often due to the aforementioned teachers but also because you may have become the only trusted adult they had in their lives. You learned the hard way about taking on too much and became better at helping others help themselves.

You discovered that there were teachers who didn't know basic teaching strategies. Had they not read Harry Wong's *The First Days of School* (2005)? You never fully comprehended that instruction was such a struggle for so many. And classroom management! Your students never acted like this in your classroom. Your consistency with appropriate and practical routines and rituals was all that was needed to successfully manage your class. The relationships you meticulously fostered never resulted in the student behaviors that you regularly found yourself helping teachers redirect.

You buckled down and talked with your principal about some new ideas and new systems for the following year. Your confidence grew, but you needed to be allowed to try a few things to help the staff and students. You needed to know whether you could experience some success as a leader of instruction and not just react to one issue after another. The principal gave you approval to employ the teacher skills that you had expertly honed to create a training on classroom management and student engagement.

Whew, you completed your first full staff training! You followed up throughout the school year with more reminders and strategies. Things were improving.

You slowly began to transition from a firefighter to the proactive stance of a lifeguard, anticipating and eliminating problems as your enhanced "AP-vision" developed.

You continued to fine-tune your ability to facilitate IEP meetings, support teachers, diffuse student recalcitrance, and have difficult, sometimes awkward conversations. Student management did not stress you anymore, and you adjusted your life to accommodate the many evenings of after-school activities and meetings. (At school athletic events, you always cheered on your students, but you slowly noticed that during volleyball games, you secretly cheered the visiting team on to win the second match if they won the first. After all, it was best of three, and you wanted to go home to your family.)

The principal gave you more responsibilities and started to teach you her systems and philosophy for staffing, scheduling, budgeting, and school leadership. You were selected to be on district leadership committees and were becoming more recognized in the community. You began to see yourself as a principal and sometimes, privately, of course, second-guessed decisions the principal made. You mastered this role, and you were eager to implement your ideas and become the salve the school needed for further improvement.

I'm Ready! Put Me In!

Once you reached this stage of confidence and readiness, you began to put yourself out there as an aspiring principal. Consequently, you began to learn a lot about school politics and practices that may or may not have been favorable to you. Maybe you knew you were ready but found yourself being overlooked time and again for a principalship. You found this phase to be a dark, lonely, confidence-busting, ego-deflating experience that tested your professionalism and emotional strength.

How did this happen to you? You recalled that the idea of being "ready" was often stoked by colleagues, staff members, family, and even your principal. After a while, you realized that you were ready, truly ready, and you confidently began applying for principal vacancies. It was when you were notified that you did not get the position that doubt crept into your confidence. And depending on who actually got the position and how much you knew about that person's readiness, it caused one of two things: it either made you double down on gaining more experiences and further fine-tuning your skills, or it started to shut down your motivation and aspiration, sending your thoughts to dark places.

If it is not obvious, I have been there. I watched peers, who I felt were equally or even less ready than I, obtain principalships and promotions while I remained the dutiful assistant principal with a toolbox overflowing with experiences and "tools" that I meticulously developed, sharpened, and honed. There are innumerable reasons that these situations may have happened, from a highly acclaimed, established principal getting the job to the more scandalous scenarios of cronyism, favoritism, or simply being overlooked.

I learned after I became the one to hire principals that there are multiple factors that go into choosing a principal. Depending on the campus and the times, it can be a high-profile decision. School board or community leaders express who they want as the next principal. Parents, students, campus reputation, sports programs, accountability standings, and/or the district's previous experience with this campus and its stakeholders are all factors that go into developing the principal candidate profile. Sometimes, it is not the most experienced or person with the best administrative qualifications but the person who will be the best fit for the campus at that moment in time.

Whether it was a short, less dramatic path or a long, dark road, eventually, you were named principal.

Part I
Becoming a Principal

2 You're Named Principal. Now What?

It was the first Saturday morning after receiving the keys, alarm code, and badge access to the high school. I wanted to take my kids to show them that one day, this would be their high school, and I was just named principal.

We entered the school and toured the halls, cafeteria, lecture room, and labs, and then we went to the gym. There were three gyms, and the third gym was divided by an industrial-grade nylon retractable screen. I never knew about this, and my kids quickly ran behind the screen and shouted, "Whoa! Dad, check this out!" It was a gymnastics gym, complete with rings, a balance beam, a pommel horse, and a huge pit with large, soft foam squares that were too much temptation for my children—and me. My kids looked at me, and I looked at them. We all smiled and instinctively jumped into the pit, laughing and screaming as we threw foam squares at each other.

As I got out and jumped to reach for the bars hanging over the pit, the school custodian walked in. I was dangling over the pit, stunned that anyone was in the building on a summer Saturday. In a stern and annoyed voice, the janitor shouted, "Hey! You are not supposed to be here. Who let you in here? Who are you?" I could no longer hold myself up on the bars, and I fell, crashing into the foam pit where I sank to the bottom. My kids were shocked into silence, and I exhausted myself trying to find my footing among the foam. I finally poked my head up and declared, "Uh, hi, I'm so sorry. I am the new principal."

DR. GOBER'S FIRST DAY ON CAMPUS

And the New Principal Is . . .

You were informed that you have been selected as the next principal. You are excited and feel accomplished. Most importantly, you start to regain the confidence that may have dwindled while you searched for this opportunity. You meet your new supervisor and are very attentive to everything that is said—the expectations, concerns, opportunities, insights about the staff, and . . . . Slowly, the magnitude of your new responsibility becomes more apparent. As your new supervisor continues to talk, showing you budgets, expressing urgency about this and that, and eventually handing you the keys, you realize the weight of the title and the level of expectations that have been set upon you. You find your inner strength and courage and do your best to convey, "I can do it!" and "No sir, you have not made a mistake."

As the news spreads, many things happen all at once. Your current campus learns that you are leaving, and the people share their support with you. Your family and friends are proud and want to celebrate. The district office starts to send you pertinent information about staffing, budgeting, scheduling, training, and other "administrivia" that you are vaguely familiar with but have never actually owned. And the staff at your new campus, the new parents, and the school community want an opportunity to meet.

The praise, the affirmation, the hope in you feels heavy, but you take it all in because you deserve it. You savor and enjoy that moment, remembering that it is okay to be proud of yourself. You are sure to thank your family, especially your spouse and children. You know they are in this with you and that they will have to sacrifice more with your new role. Yes, you need to prepare the family.

Prepare Your Family and Remember to Put Them First!

I believe that the principal's family is the most overlooked and underappreciated stakeholder of the campus. Whether you live within the campus boundaries or not, your family is an important part of your success and thus the success of that campus. As principal, you need to fully understand not only the role your family has but also the sacrifices they will have to endure.

If you have a spouse or children, they gain new titles that they tolerate more than covet. They become the "principal's kids" and the "principal's husband or wife." They may endure a certain level of scrutiny depending on the community and profile of the campus. When you or your family are in public, there may be people looking at you and talking about you. There may be people taking pictures. It sounds fascinating until it is not. A moment of indiscretion can land you, and possibly them, in the newspaper or, worse, at the center of the latest social media gossip. If your children are school-aged, they will be expected to have stellar grades, exemplary manners, and, of course, be the model student at their school. Quadruple that expectation if they attend your school.

Right or wrong, there are higher expectations for not only you but also your family. You know this and signed up for it, but your family needs to be fully informed and aware because they indirectly signed up too.

Your family will endure more than just judgments about outward appearances. You will inevitably be absent from home and family events. They got a taste of it while you were assistant principal, but it does not get better when you are principal. For all these reasons and countless more, you need to always thank your family and help prepare them for this new role. Understanding all of this makes it even more imperative that you create a school environment that is highly efficient, effective, and positive so that you can spend time with your family and maintain a happy and healthy home.

The "OH CRAP" Moment

This moment usually arrives the same day you go to your new campus on a late evening or an early Saturday to set things up. You finish setting up your professional yet approachable office, carefully selecting the optimal place to put your family photos. You sit down, admiring your talent as an interior decorator (or you send a text to your wife for help). You look at your desk and the photo of your family and reflect for a moment. You begin to recall your notes from the meeting when you were hired and pull them out, and that's when the floodgates open. You log into your computer, then your email, and OH CRAP, there are a ton of messages just waiting on you!

There are congratulations and welcome messages, meeting requests, deadlines, and reminders from the district, applicants looking for jobs, an upcoming training you need to attend, vendor solicitations, and a complaint from a teacher about something the previous principal did to her schedule. Wait, there are a few more complaints—from parents, staff, and the neighbor across the street from the school who hopes you don't have fire drills before 9:00 a.m. because he works midnights. You didn't notice these as complaints at first because they were embedded as welcome or congratulatory messages. Oh, there's a lovely message from a staff member who informs you that she always helps with all the back-to-school planning and is available to meet whenever you come up for air.

You want to make a difference; you want to show the campus (and yourself) that hiring you was not a mistake. You want to be the best principal ever, so what do you do? You do what every principal before you has done: you quickly respond to all of the district emails and inquiries so that the district office knows you have everything under control.

Your OH CRAP moment cannot last long, and it certainly cannot be seen by anyone else. You don't even want to admit to yourself that you had it. So, you instinctively dive into the work as best you know how, trying to show that you are poised, professional, and confident (but not too confident) in all your emails and messages. You went to the office only planning to set it up and prepare for your first day, but you are the principal now, and you need to show everyone that you are ready, willing, and able to do this job. So, the short-lived admiration of your office turns into a flurry of email responses: you write brief thank-you notes to all those who welcomed and congratulated you. You decide to wait until the next day to respond to those other messages. You want to think more carefully about how to respond, and you want to get back home to your daughter's soccer game before you get too immersed in the new role.

But wait! You want everyone to see that you are responsive. So, you respond to all your emails, thinking it best to start your official first day with an empty inbox. Two hours later, you head for home. You think to yourself, "It's not so bad. I know what to do. I just need to stay on top of things." Inadvertently, you just told yourself that you are going to do what has always been done. Yes, you might make some tweaks here and there. Yes, you might move some staff members and hire some superstars. And yes, you are committed to being more visible and engaged than the previous principal, but no, you don't really have a plan. You don't really have the systems that you need mapped out and ready to implement.

And you finally drive home, realizing that you missed your daughter's soccer game and dinner with the family.

Do not worry, and certainly do not feel you are unworthy of this position. Most principals, especially new principals, knowingly or unknowingly, take the safe road that they have experienced as a teacher and AP and do what the campus has always done.

The longer the principal is in that role, the more confident they become that their campus is the "smoothest sailing ship in the sea." As the new principal, you don't always know who preceded you or their level of effectiveness. Many believe it would be easy to follow a principal who had effective systems in place, a positive school culture, and exemplary safety and security measures with high student academic performance. However, those who have been in that situation will share that although it is great to inherit a school that is not in disrepair, it is hard to get out of the shadow of that principal. Conversely, your predecessor could have been a micromanager or complete *laissez-faire* type of leader who was not well received by stakeholders. In these cases, or when inheriting a campus with low student academic growth and achievement, you become the "great hope" for the campus. These scenarios, and the hundreds in between, have pros and cons. Before you go in and start making changes, you first need to learn about who was there and how things work.

3 Learn About What You Have Inherited

It is what it is, until it isn't.
EVERY NEW PRINCIPAL WHO WANTS TO CHANGE THE STATUS QUO.

Leadership expert and author Warren Bennis (2009) proclaims that "A manager accepts the status quo, a leader challenges it." However, a leader cannot effectively challenge the status quo without first understanding it. First impressions are critical—they shape how others perceive us, often leading to lasting generalizations. You do not want to expend valuable time correcting misconceptions, as this inherently positions you in a defensive leadership posture. Instead, it is essential to acknowledge and celebrate the accomplishments and strengths of the campus and its staff upon arrival. Your initial actions on campus can either establish you as a manager or position you as a true leader.

The Transition

Some new principals are fortunate enough to follow a principal who left a transition document or plan. This can be a meeting or a letter welcoming you and telling you who is who and what is what. If you are really fortunate, that principal will leave their files: org charts, staff trainings, letter templates, calendars, master schedules, newsletter templates, and the most recent school data. These types of transition documents are very helpful as you start to unravel the intricacies of how this school works. You need to discover who the leaders are, both formally and informally, what the norms are, and where the landmines and closets with skeletons hide.

Do not forget the importance of transition documents when you someday leave that campus for a new role or retirement. Transition notes, files, and documents will save your successor a lot of headaches and add to your legacy as an outstanding principal. I inherited three campuses, and only one principal gave me transition files. It was the motherlode in the form of a thumb drive that contained every document a budding principal would ever need. I am forever grateful to that principal, and I cite him as a mentor in my dedication.

Two Ears, One Mouth

Whether you receive transition documents or not, you are still going to give proper regard to the old adage that God gave you two ears and one mouth. Listen and learn. Listen to everyone. Everyone will want to meet with you and learn more about you. Your job in these early days consists of listening, learning, and *promising nothing*.

When you start to meet with stakeholders, many will ask questions that demand more than an answer—they want a commitment. For example, "Mr. New Principal, what are you going to do about the tardy problem?" or "What is your vision for the campus?" Be slow to answer and never feel like you absolutely have to answer any question right then and there. Stay broad and high to give yourself time to develop the details that they really want.

Some of these questions are not questions at all. They are posed as a question but really signal a concern. For example, "What do you think of the new curriculum?" or "Do you schedule yourself for lunch duty?" Some people will do this to test you, and others will do it to be helpful. Fight the temptation to show that you have the answers. Fight the temptation to instantly win over the staff or gain standing ovations from parents by making promises when you do not know the full context of the question or have not had the time to set priorities for the campus.

If you answer questions the way they want you to answer, such as, "We will not tolerate students being in the halls after the bell rings, and those who are tardy to class will be held accountable," you will inadvertently set priorities for your first year as principal. Maybe you would have landed on that anyway, but do not let poor preparation and the temptation to gain approval set your priorities before you get the full lay of the land.

Have a notebook and take notes on everything being shared with you at all your meetings and interactions. You want to do this starting the day you are named principal. You need to set up some meetings—be proactive and go

A/V Studio
Advanced Academics
AP
AP Courses
Assessment Calendar
Athletics
Attendance
Book Studies
Boosters
BOY Presentations
Budgets
Bullying Prevention
Campus Images
Campus Profile
Clubs and Organizations
College Tours
Community Outreach
Community Resources
Construction
Contract Renewal
Counselors
Course List
Course Proposal
Credit Recovery
CTE
Curriculum – District
Custodial and Maintenance
Dances
Data – Campus/District
Data – Historical
Data – Student
Data – Teacher Effect
Data Team
Department Chairs
Differentiation
Digital Citizenship
Discipline Committee
District Forms and Letters

District Information
Diversity
Dress Code
Drug Awareness
Due Process Hearings
Duty Schedules
ELA – Reading
Eligibility
Emergency Procedures
Enrollment Projections
EOY Procedures
Expulsions
Faculty Council
Field Trips
Final Exams
Fine Arts
First Day of School
Free/Reduced Lunch
Freshman Orientation
Fundraisers
Gifted Talented
GPA
Grading Guidelines
Graduation Requirements
Hiring Materials
Homebound Services
Homecoming
IB – DP
IB – MYP
Icebreakers
Inspiration
Instructional Coaches
Instructional Snapshots
Interpreters
Interview Questions
Job Descriptions
JROTC
Leadership Team

Lesson Planning
Letter Templates
Library
Lockers
Logos
LOTE
Lunches
Maps / Floorplans
Master Schedule
Math
Medical Forms
Mental Health
Mission Vision
Monday Memos
MTSS
Murals
New AP Orientation
New Teacher Orientation
Newsletters
NHS
Nurse
Onboarding
Open House
Parent Night
Parent Conferences
Parking
Partnerships
PE
Peer Tutoring
Picture Day
PLC Schedules
PLC Training
Presidents Council
Principal Appraisal
Principal Council
Principal Meetings – District
Professional Learning
Prom

PTA
Recycling
Religious Holidays
Resumes
Retention Schedule
Safety Security
Schedule Changes
School Board
Science
Site Calendar
Social Studies
Special Education
Special Events
Staff Projections
STEAM
Stipends
Student Advisory
Student Code of Conduct
Student Council
Student Handbook
Student Registration
Suicide Outcry Guidelines
Summer Graduation
Summer School
Surveys
Teacher Appraisals
Team Leaders
Technology
Transfer Students
Transportation
Travel – Admin
Travel – Staff
Travel – Student
Unit Planners
Vacancy Reports
Volunteers
Webmaster
Yearbook

Figure 3.1 Screenshot of principal transition files.

to them before they come to you. Have a meet and greet for the entire staff and a separate one for students, parents, and community.

You cannot individually meet with everyone, but I would suggest scheduling one-on-ones with the following stakeholders:

- District leaders
- Assistant principals
- Secretary/administrative assistant
- Counselor(s)
- Lead custodian
- Teacher leaders
- Parent leaders
- Student leaders

Listen and take notes from each stakeholder meeting. For your meet-and-greets and larger meetings, talk about your career path, a little about your family, your hobbies, your passion as an educator, your "why," and your excitement to learn all the great things about this school and its students. Be excited, high energy, confident, and genuine, *but do not be arrogant*. This is all that is expected of you. You will be asked many questions; some will be broad, and others will be very specific. Remember, stay disciplined—do not fall for the trap! Stay positive, energetic, and open. Give yourself the time to learn about your leadership team, build trust, and process all that you have heard.

Everything comes at you in those first weeks like water from a firehose; you can make sense of it all by condensing your notes to short lists of bullets divided by the stakeholder group it came from (see Figure 3.2).

Another strategy is to take all of your notes and divide them by topics (see Figure 3.3).

From your lists, you should now be able to see the areas that require your attention. You can begin to prioritize a "To Do" list with urgent matters on top. To prioritize, I look at what categories have the most notes or comments. Having the most comments or becoming the "squeaky wheel" does not necessarily mean it will become a high priority, but it is definitely an area that you need to address sooner rather than later. Finally, be realistic: items directed as priorities by district leaders are obviously going to the top, but the complaint about the early morning fire drills is just a concern and can wait.

Many of these tasks deserve a subsystem or protocol because they are routine or ongoing, and addressing them should not become a huge ordeal every year. Use the existing protocols to tackle this to-do list if such a protocol already exists. Doing so will garner some trust from the staff, who may think you are going to change everything from the start.

It's okay to ask your APs and secretary to help you tackle all of this. Trust me, most are dying to show you how competent and reliable they are. On the flip side, you may encounter resistance because they are not happy you are there, and they have decided they will not make your life easy. Either way, it is good to know these things early.

As you begin to work with the existing protocols, be sure to find opportunities to make small improvements and to recognize existing efficiencies. You are establishing what your "presence" entails. Take time to think through this—do

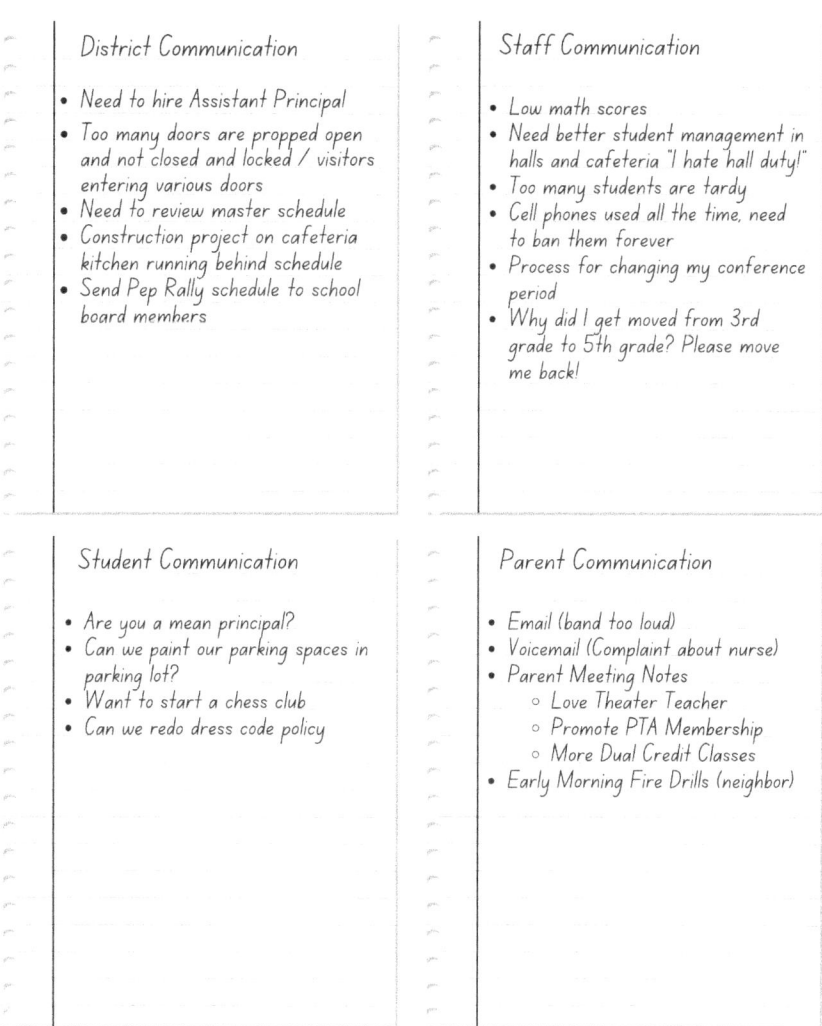

District Communication

- Need to hire Assistant Principal
- Too many doors are propped open and not closed and locked / visitors entering various doors
- Need to review master schedule
- Construction project on cafeteria kitchen running behind schedule
- Send Pep Rally schedule to school board members

Staff Communication

- Low math scores
- Need better student management in halls and cafeteria "I hate hall duty!"
- Too many students are tardy
- Cell phones used all the time, need to ban them forever
- Process for changing my conference period
- Why did I get moved from 3rd grade to 5th grade? Please move me back!

Student Communication

- Are you a mean principal?
- Can we paint our parking spaces in parking lot?
- Want to start a chess club
- Can we redo dress code policy

Parent Communication

- Email (band too loud)
- Voicemail (Complaint about nurse)
- Parent Meeting Notes
  - Love Theater Teacher
  - Promote PTA Membership
  - More Dual Credit Classes
- Early Morning Fire Drills (neighbor)

Figure 3.2 Communication notes by stakeholder.

you want your presence to be welcomed and valued, or do you want your name and presence to instill fear and resentment like Mufasa from Disney's *The Lion King*? The **Principal Presence** I subscribe to trusts, welcomes, and receives people and ideas with positive intent. It includes a willingness to help, share, and work with everyone. Do not go in and point out everything that is wrong or share everything that you know; doing so can be fatal to the success of your principalship. Two ears, one mouth! Learn how the campus operates and accept how they do things. Always highlight an efficient or

Academics:	Climate/Culture:	Student Management:
• Departments	• Safety and Security	• Classroom Behavior
• Growth	• Sense of Belonging	• Campus Behavior
• Performance	• School Pride	• Consequences /
	• Staff/Student	Actions
	Morale	

Parents:	Student Activities:	Staffing / Personnel:
• Complaints	• Clubs	• Vacant Positions
• Engagement	• Teams	• Vacant Leader
• Suggestions	• Coaches/Sponsors	Positions
• Volunteers	• Yearbook	• Role/Schedule Changes

Figure 3.3 Communication notes by topic.

effective practice. You have plenty of time to make changes, but making those changes will be more difficult if your presence is not welcome.

Principal Honeymoons Are Short, So SWOT Early

Principal "honeymoon periods" exist, but they are fleeting. During the initial phase of your principalship, you are often viewed favorably, and it is crucial not to squander this brief window on minor tasks or procedural changes. It is far more impactful to take the time to understand the existing systems and assess their effectiveness. By changing a system without fully understanding it, you risk implementing something even less effective. Thoughtful, informed changes have greater potential for lasting improvement.

Although your honeymoon will often be interrupted with "slaps" of reality, such as a disgruntled teacher, an upset parent, or the discovery that anyone will park in the "Reserved Parking—Principal" spot, you need to capitalize on this opportunity to learn the professional culture of the school. As the new principal, you need a fast yet effective way to understand the school's current position and make informed decisions for its future. In their book, *SWOT*

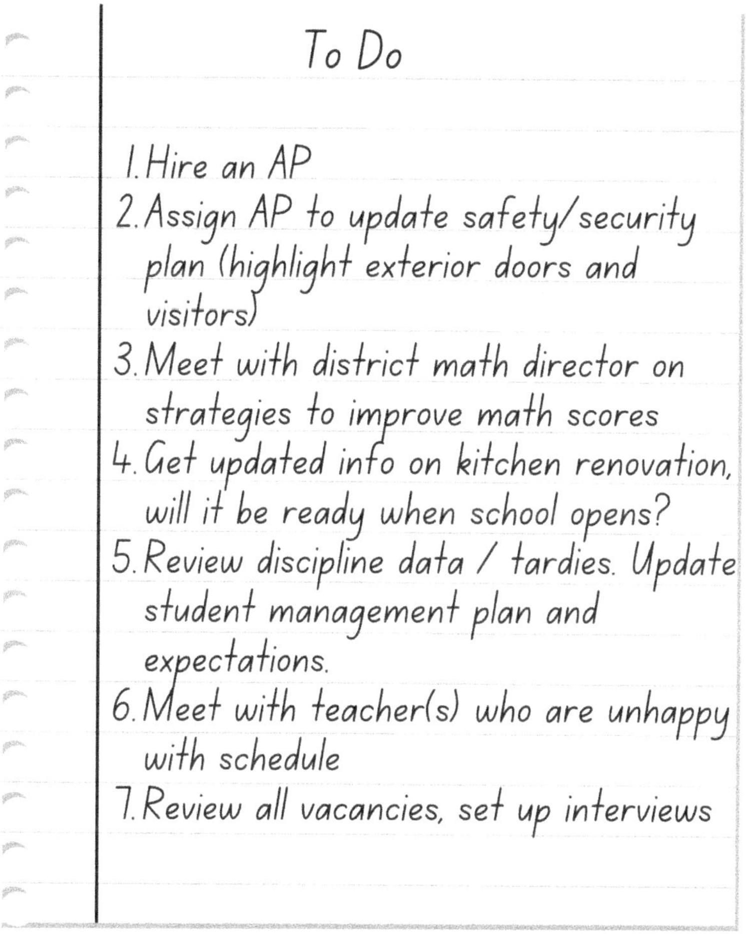

To Do

1. Hire an AP
2. Assign AP to update safety/security plan (highlight exterior doors and visitors)
3. Meet with district math director on strategies to improve math scores
4. Get updated info on kitchen renovation, will it be ready when school opens?
5. Review discipline data / tardies. Update student management plan and expectations.
6. Meet with teacher(s) who are unhappy with schedule
7. Review all vacancies, set up interviews

Figure 3.4 Communication notes by priority—to-do list.

Analysis: Idea, Methodology, and a Practical Approach, Nicole Pahl and Anne Richter (2009) describe SWOT analysis as a strategic planning tool used to assess an organization's internal strengths and weaknesses as well as external opportunities and threats. The SWOT tool is well known in both business and school settings and will be the theme for your honeymoon.

Whether you are hired over the summer or in the middle of a school year, this tool works. I strongly recommend giving the staff the option to complete the SWOT anonymously because, at this moment, they don't trust you and may not be as transparent when citing weaknesses and threats. Sending an email to the staff asking for their feedback will likely earn you trust and

Dear Team,

I'm excited to work with you to build an exceptional school for our students and community. As the new guy, I'm eager to learn from you about what's working well and where we can improve.

To help me better understand our school, please complete a SWOT analysis (Strengths, Weaknesses, Opportunities, and Threats). Feel free to share any insights or feedback you believe would help us create an action plan that:
- Strengthens our core assets
- Addresses key weaknesses
- Seizes growth opportunities
- Protects us from internal and external threats

Thank you for your support and partnership. I look forward to a fantastic year ahead!

Best regards,
Dr. G

Figure 3.5 Sample email to staff.

support, which is essential for your success as a principal. You can apply the information you glean from it to later enhance your **Principal Mystique**. Figure 3.5 is an email you can use.

Using a technology tool like Google Forms can make it easy for both the staff to complete the analysis and for you to review the results.

Now you have the gold mine of feedback from your staff. With the feedback you gained from your other stakeholders, you have enough fodder to assess where to focus your efforts for necessary change. It is best to obtain this feedback as early as possible. You are going to want to make some changes, and you could very innocently make a change that will not be well received. Listen and learn, and don't forget that principals have short honeymoons.

4 The Role of the Principal

Principals without systems are like teachers without lesson plans.
DR. GOBER

Established Roles in Current School Leadership

I am not such a cynic as to think that there is nothing new to learn in education, but I do lean toward this view when it comes to school leadership. Prior to the 2021 Wallace study, school leadership was generally defined around twenty roles and responsibilities. I grouped these into five overarching categories, highlighting the key attributes of each group:

1. **Instructional Leadership and Curriculum Development** (Leithwood et al., 2008; Fullan, 2001)

    This category focuses on ensuring high-quality teaching and learning.

    ● Curriculum planning and development

    ● Instructional strategies and best practices

    ● Professional development for teachers

    ● Monitoring and assessing student progress

    ● Integration of technology into teaching and learning

2. **School Management and Operations** (Hallinger, 2003; Harris et al., 2003)

    This category deals with the administrative and operational aspects of the school.

    ● Budgeting and financial management

    ● Human resources management (staff recruitment, development, and evaluation)

    ● Facilities management and maintenance

    ● Safety and security protocols

    ● Compliance with regulations and policies

3. **Student Support and Well-Being** (Bryk and Schneider, 2002; Center for Mental Health in Schools at UCLA, n.d.)

   This category focuses on supporting the social, emotional, and physical well-being of students.

   - Counseling and guidance services
   - Special education and learning support services
   - Health and wellness programs
   - Behavior management and discipline policies
   - Crisis management and intervention strategies

4. **Community and Stakeholder Engagement** (Sergiovanni, 1996; Epstein, 2001)

   This category involves building and maintaining positive relationships with stakeholders inside and outside the school community.

   - Communication strategies with parents, guardians, and the broader community
   - Collaboration with local businesses, organizations, and educational partners
   - Parent involvement and volunteer programs
   - Public relations and community outreach efforts
   - Alumni relations and fundraising activities

5. **Data Management and Assessment** (DuFour et al., 2016; Marzano et al., 2005)

   This category focuses on collecting, analyzing, and using data to inform decision-making and improve student outcomes.

   - Student data tracking and analysis (academic performance, attendance, behavior)
   - Assessment and evaluation of school programs and initiatives
   - Use of data to identify areas for improvement and set goals
   - Reporting and communicating data to stakeholders
   - Continuous improvement processes based on data-driven insights

Each role listed above has hundreds of well-written articles, books, and research-driven workshops for principals to explore and use to enhance their proverbial toolbox. I do not pretend to be an expert in all of the roles. However, there are five areas that I have found that, once mastered and implemented with fidelity, bring about an effective school. Why only five? Because when principals are faced with twenty, they become overwhelmed, and any notion of implementation at that point is done as a matter of compliance.

There are also two assumptions I make that allow me to focus on only five areas. First, I know that each area is the primary role or focus of someone else on my team or in the district—for example, the district's curriculum development; and second, I know I have subsystems in place that are monitored within my five primary systems. Those five systems are Communication, Collaboration, Lesson Planning, Instructional Snapshots, and Data Monitoring. But before we get into those systems, we need to be realistic about what is in the realm of our control. Let's discuss principal autonomy.

Leveraging Autonomy as a Principal

School districts often centralize decisions, limiting the autonomy of individual campuses in areas like curriculum development, professional development, safety, and technology. Districts typically deploy specialists to create standardized programs and protocols for campuses to follow, ensuring consistency across the board. Even in cases where districts don't fully mandate specific practices, they still offer significant support to campuses, reinforcing district-wide expectations. This creates a structured environment, though it can reduce the decision making flexibility of individual principals.

Most principals have a small role in the development and management of these systems, and I have been fortunate (or sometimes unfortunate) enough to be a part of school districts that provided these supports. Where districts are too small to offer all of these services, there is usually a regional or state office or specialist to provide the needed assistance or support.

As a principal, I needed to know how much autonomy I truly had over these school leadership areas. Sometimes, that autonomy was crystal clear in areas such as budgeting, curriculum development, and personnel management. Other times, it depended on how "centralized" the district leaders were, and over time those leaders changed. With one superintendent, I had to ensure that the federal- and state-mandated trainings were provided to my staff. Other than that, I had complete autonomy over my staff's professional development. With another superintendent, I was given the presentation slides with a written script that I had to follow for every staff training that came from the district.

Since I could not control these things, I chose to focus on things that I could control. For the most part, I have always understood that my role was *to create a positive and productive school culture that emanates high expectations for student achievement by engaging in instructionally focused interactions with teachers, facilitating productive collaboration, and strategically managing school resources*. Note the parallel with the four principal behaviors that produced positive school outcomes as explained in the 2021 Wallace research: focusing on instruction in their interactions with teachers, building a productive school climate, promoting collaboration and professional learning among teachers and others, and managing personnel and resources well.

To fulfill my role as I understood it, I had to find a way to incorporate best practices as described and researched by top scholars. Again, I am not about to outline anything new, profound, or groundbreaking. I am, however, going to show you how to implement these best practices as systems that are clear to your stakeholders, manageable for you, and sustainable for the campus.

Five Systems for an Effective School— An Overview

Communication

First, and this is perhaps the most visible to all stakeholders, you need a system for communication. Merriam-Webster's Dictionary (n.d.) defines communication as a process by which information is exchanged. Our communication system will focus on how the principal disseminates information. It will also outline tools and school organization designed to move information in and out of the organization and up and down within the school.

I have always thought that the root causes of most school problems usually lie in some sort of breakdown in communication. As we embark upon a new era of technology and artificial intelligence (AI), I asked ChatGPT, an open-source

AI platform, this question: "What is the root cause of most of the world's problems?" The response: "The most common root cause for most problems, across various contexts and situations, often boils down to communication issues" (OpenAI, personal communication, July 2, 2024).

But if you do not want to believe my hunch or AI's findings on the importance of an effective communication system, consider reading *Leadership and Organizational Behavior in Education: Theory into Practice* (Owings and Kaplan, 2013). It provides excellent case studies and personal experiences on how communication breakdowns lead to problems in educational settings.

Collaboration—PLCs

Hopefully, our next system will not be a stranger to you or your district—collaboration. In 2006, Rick Dufour transformed instruction and instructional leadership with the publication *Learning by Doing: A Handbook for Professional Learning Communities at Work*. Dufour's work describes the difference between a group of teachers meeting or planning and a group of teachers collaborating about instruction, using data, and asking essential questions, thus forming a Professional Learning Community (PLC).

It is not my intent to convince you how powerfully PLCs can improve student academic achievement. That work has been done repeatedly, and if you still refuse to implement a formal structure for teachers to meet regularly to improve their practice and enhance student learning, please stop reading. I am not only promoting PLCs but also the idea that the principal has an active role (**Principal Presence**) in PLCs by providing feedback on a regular basis. Your first thought may be that this is too much, but Chapter 7, "Collaboration," will explain why the feedback is important, and Chapter 12, "Your Time" will show you how to make the time to get it all done.

Lesson Planning

For most of my career, I have strongly advocated for the importance of lesson planning. The traditional Madeline Hunter-style lesson plan was a great tool to focus and align instruction to learning objectives. But if you lived through the days of completing those lesson plans, you knew them to be laborious, time-consuming, and oftentimes just an act of compliance. As a principal, I expected lesson plans but admittedly did not inspect them. However, I have evolved as an administrator, and with advancing technology, I have become much more flexible. How teachers complete lesson plans is much less important than the evidence of sound instructional planning and the ability of students and parents to see their teacher's instructional roadmap. I still believe in lesson plans, but I believe in smart lesson plans that are teacher-friendly and relevant for students, parents, and teachers. I also have learned the importance of providing feedback on lesson plans. Initially, I struggled to provide feedback consistently. I needed a system to monitor (**Principal Mystique**) and interact (**Principal Presence**) with our teachers' instructional planning. This is another behavior that produces positive school outcomes, as outlined in the 2021 Wallace study, "Engaging in instructionally focused interactions with teachers" (Grissom et al., 2021, p. xv).

Managing and Monitoring Data

I needed a system to manage and monitor our data. What data? Exactly my point! There was so much data that I mistakenly assumed that my teachers or district staff were analyzing everything and making the adjustments or providing recommendations necessary for improvement. I could not be an expert on all the assessments my campus rolled out, and I certainly could not manage, analyze, and synthesize all of the data that was needed to truly make a difference. Thanks to technology, we no longer need to carry heavy binders of student rosters with tiny numbers next to them. I taught my teachers how to access and analyze data and created a data team to help me become a data-informed decision-maker for my campus.

The Instructional Snapshot

I once was asked, "What does instruction look like on your campus?" The educational consultant was not asking a trick question and certainly was not expecting me to look as dumbfounded as I was, but I babbled away about how we strive to provide relevant, engaging instruction to meet the differing needs of all our students. Little did I know that there was a follow-up question to rub the polish from my pride: "How do you know if this type of instruction is happening in all of your classrooms?" That was, how did I know if my teachers were providing relevant, engaging instruction to meet the differing needs of all our students? WHAT? Being the seasoned educator that I was, I explained our teacher evaluation system, complete with observation and walkthrough protocols. To which the consultant said, "Hmm, ok."

I learned more from that consultant, and why wouldn't I? Dr. Phil Warrick, an experienced high school principal, author, and researcher at The Marzano Institute, was auditing my campus to determine our status as a High Reliability School®. Dr. Warrick went on to explain the type of evidence and artifacts that would help me determine what instruction looked like on my campus. He described multiple things, but I was stuck on what he called "instructional snapshots": brief, non-evaluative, tailor-made walkthroughs that listed instructional "look-fors" that my campus leaders and I would agree that we expected to see in every classroom during instruction. We now had a tool, and we soon created a system so we would always know if we were measuring up to what we believed instruction should look like at our school.

5 First Things First— Organize Your Organization

Give me six hours to chop down a tree, and I will spend the first four sharpening the ax.
ABRAHAM LINCOLN

The principal must make time to plan and have a system to retrieve and disseminate information and, most importantly, monitor all systems. Before we can discuss systems in more detail, we must put some structure to this complex organization. Most likely, there will be an established structure that you should learn and learn fast. But you are the principal; if that structure is not going to meet your needs, this is a good opportunity to implement a change.

When educators discuss planning, they are often referring to teachers. But planning is equally important for the principal. Most principals who inherit an established campus do little to change the existing staff structure. Some even use the status quo as an excuse for not making necessary changes because "that's not how we do things here." Campus organization is a key component to successfully implement and operate your systems. For example, a clear, consistent, and practical structure must be developed for information to move from the principal to the stakeholders and vice versa. The system for the flow of information, otherwise known as communication, needs to provide ease and speed as well as offer opportunities for stakeholders to remain anonymous.

Organize Your Staff

Let's start with organizing our staff into Collaborative Teams (PLCs), Operational Teams (departments), and Functional Teams (noninstructional campus level teams such as counselors or administrators).

Elementary schools have a long tradition of having grade-level teams. If the elementary does not "departmentalize" or have specific teachers teaching specific content, the Collaborative Team also serves as the Operational Team. Their time together is given purpose based on how that time is scheduled. For example, the second-grade team meets every Tuesday at 9:00 a.m. for collaboration or PLC time. But after school, on the second and fourth Thursdays of the month, there is the second-grade Operations meeting (department meeting). I would be cautious about mixing operations with collaboration during a set meeting time. Collaboration (PLC) meetings have a specific agenda that includes spending time looking at artifacts and data while planning the assessments and the instruction that follows. Discussing specific students, interventions, and lesson extensions all take a lot of time, and this time to collaborate should be held sacred. Operation meetings are for all of the other administrative tasks and planning that need to occur.

How to treat your elective or "specials" teachers is a decision that becomes difficult primarily due to scheduling. Some administrators create a pseudo-PLC of elective teachers, while others may assign an elective teacher to one of the grade levels, and some do not assign them to any Collaborative (PLC) Team but include them on the campus leadership team. Figure 5.1 shows an example of the latter and how staff members may be represented at each level.

Scenario: I am a first-grade teacher; I am a member of the campus staff. I also belong to the 1st Grade PLC, which has a separate Grade-Level/Operations meeting twice a month after school. The first-grade team leader is a member of the Campus Leadership Team, and there is an AP assigned to the first-grade

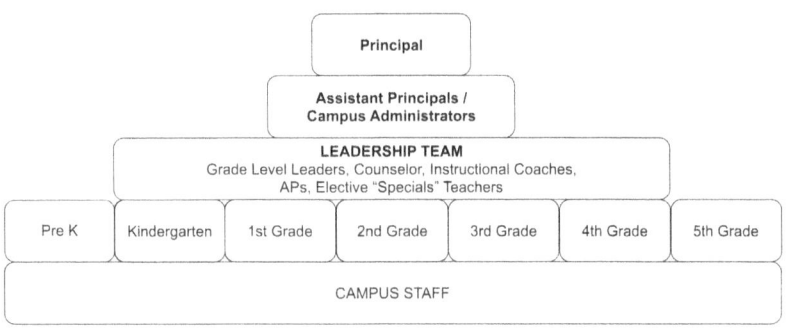

Figure 5.1 Elementary staff organization.

team who meets weekly with our principal and other campus administrators at the Admin Team Meeting. Our AP regularly attends our PLCs and visits our classrooms, so he is very familiar with what is happening in first grade.

This type of structure ensures that everyone not only has a sense of belonging but also that the challenges, celebrations, and needs of each staff member can be addressed with their colleagues, campus leaders, and principal. Now, let's push something down to see how that works.

The district office shared at the last principals' meeting that each campus needed to implement the newly purchased character education program on Friday afternoons next month as part of the "Friendly Fridays" campaign to counter bullying. As a result, each campus is to create a modified schedule for the four Fridays of the month that allows for a dedicated two-hour block on character education to focus on bullying prevention.

The principal discusses this with the other administrators at the Monday morning Admin Team meeting and assigns one of the APs to be the point person for this project. During the meeting, the Admin Team reviews and makes minor revisions to the district's sample schedule and short presentation to prepare for the Leadership Team meeting later that day. At the Campus Leadership Team meeting, they present the "what and why" (character education lessons that focus on the prevention of bullying to carry out the district's "Friendly Fridays" campaign); the Campus Leadership Team discusses the "when, where, and how" afterward with sample schedules. They look over the dates and times, discuss the procedures, request a few modifications, and finalize a plan. This plan is discussed at their Grade Level or Operations meetings and is also highlighted in the weekly Monday Memo (a tool used as a portable staff meeting), where the principal directs staff to alter instructional plans in their upcoming PLC meetings. Furthermore, the "Friendly Fridays" plan is posted on the campus calendar, which is published in the weekly Campus Newsletter and on the campus website for the parents and public to see.

The staff have now heard about the plan at least three times and can see the dates on the campus calendar and school website. That includes three touch points for the "Friendly Fridays" plan. If a teacher has concerns, she can share them with her team leader or AP to be brought up at the next leadership meeting. If it is an urgent concern, that teacher can immediately email the principal, being sure to copy her assistant principal and team leader. Let's take a look at a secondary school.

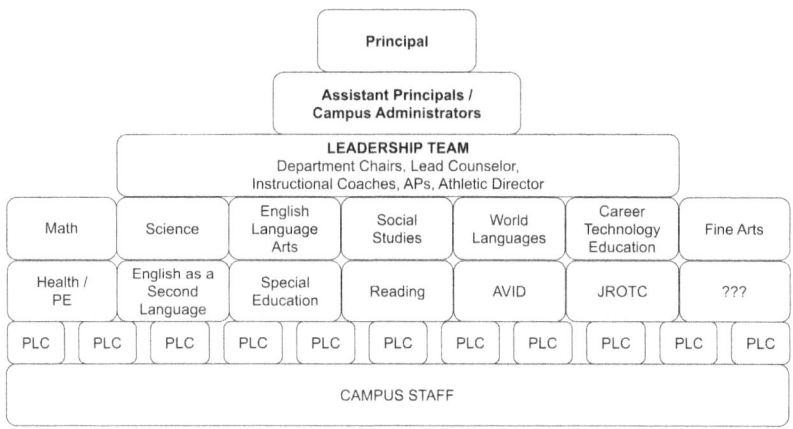

Figure 5.2 Secondary staff organization.

A secondary school can easily have upward of forty PLCs. To ensure we know how the PLCs relate to the department, let's zoom in on the math department. We will also look at a PLC with only one teacher, such as a statistics teacher, and PLCs that also belong to other departments, such as IEP Math and Emergent Bilingual (EB) Math.

The math department has eleven different content areas. Each one requires time for those content area teachers to collaborate. However, two of those content areas have only one teacher—Trigonometry and Statistics. Those two teachers would not be assigned to a PLC unless they teach in another content area that does have a PLC. Two areas are included in another department—EB Math and IEP Math. Administration and teachers should collaboratively decide whether these EB and Special Education teachers belong to two departments (i.e., Special Education and Math) or one.

Rarely will anything at any school look so neat and clean, so let's add some more realities. It is quite possible to have a department of one. Junior Reserve Officers' Training Corps (JROTC), Advancement Via Individual Determination (AVID), and sometimes even Career and Technical Education (CTE) content areas can have one staff member. Depending on how many of these singleton departments you have, you may want to combine a few. This helps your leadership team stay manageable and gives everyone a team to belong to. In this example, I would merge my JROTC instructor with Health/PE or with CTE and my AVID teacher with ELA. When CTE is a singleton, it's best to put it with another elective. Another option would be to take all of them and create an "elective department."

What if we have a baseball coach who teaches Algebra 1, Calculus, and Physical Education (PE)? For PLC assignments, my rule of thumb is that if a teacher is teaching in the four core content areas and that area has other teachers, then they need to be in that PLC. However, if they are split between two content areas and one is a state accountability area, then they PLC with the area that is state assessed. So, the baseball coach will belong to the math department and the Algebra 1 PLC because Algebra 1 is a state-tested area.

There are infinite ways to divide up staff; the important thing is to have a plan that is practical, sustainable, and implemented with consistency. Every year, there will be a new anomaly. This is inevitable, and you should not need to create a new exception—you have a system for this. Every staff member belongs to a department; if more than one teacher is in a content area, then a PLC exists. The work of a PLC does not go away when a PLC does not exist—those PLC essential questions should be considered in the development of every teacher's weekly lesson plan.

Staff is by far the most complicated group to organize because there are a lot of technical implications such as appraisals, budgets, and master schedules. Organizing our parents and students is easier because the structure focuses primarily on communication.

Who Takes Care of the Parents and Community?

Communicating effectively involves numerous skills and structures that have been researched and written about by hundreds of scholars in thousands of books and articles. When it comes to school principals communicating with parents or the community at large, It really is quite simple: be proactive, relevant, and timely. To achieve this, we must spread the burden and create not only capacity but also expertise in certain areas.

As a new high school principal, I was not well versed in the intricacies of cheerleading, and this group of parents required a lot of attention. From tryouts, game-day expectations, field trips, and various competitions, the parents always brought concerns to me that I simply did not know how to answer. However, I had an assistant principal who was a former cheer coach. She understood much better than I what was being asked (or not asked) by this group of parents. She became the point of contact for this group of parents to effectively provide the proactive, relevant, and timely communication we all needed.

Over the years, my knowledge base and comfort level in discussing cheerleader matters grew, as did my knowledge and comfort level with band, choir, athletics, agriculture, and the culinary program. However, even if I were an expert in all of these areas, I don't believe I could be as responsive to the concerns that were regularly brought up as they deserved. Dividing the parent organizations among my Admin Team was essential to the success of my communication system.

> I believe strongly in the impact a well-run Parent Teacher Association (PTA) can have on a campus and school community. The strength and influence of a PTA can be a good or a bad thing. I never wanted to leave this to chance, and I also wanted to show how much I believed in this organization by attending every meeting and event and having monthly meetings with the PTA president. This is one parent organization I did not delegate; this is the primary parent organization, and as such, it deserves the primary attention from the primary administrator—the principal.

> Due to my belief in this organization, I always ensured that we had 100% staff participation. I could count on the PTA to provide a back-to-school luncheon, holiday dinner, or teacher appreciation meal, among other events. I encouraged the staff to join PTA by saying to them, "Don't eat PTA food if you don't pay PTA dues." This phrase became an annual joke-but-not-joking staple at our beginning-of-the-year staff meeting. We always had 100% staff participation.

The other nonnegotiable I had involved community and civic organizations. I will admit that my involvement with these organizations varied depending on the district's expectations and the existing community culture. But the high school principal of a one-high-school town de facto becomes a community leader with higher status than one might expect. I quickly learned the importance of my presence at the meetings or events held by these organizations. I either attended or had regular contact with Rotary International, Lions Clubs International, National Association for the Advancement of Colored People, League of United Latin American Citizens, and other civic and community-based organizations important to each specific community.

I needed to spread my **Principal Presence** to all of the parents and community organizations, so I used the structure in Figure 5.3.

In Chapter 6, "Communication," I will go more in depth about how, when, and what to communicate with parent and community stakeholders.

Nurture Your Students

It is my belief that every student should belong to a club, team, or school organization. I would promote this heavily at the beginning of the school year, especially at "Fish Camp," or freshmen orientation. "We have over 30 clubs, and if we don't have a club you want, come talk to me about forming a new club." When students belong to a club or team (including athletics, band, choir, orchestra, and theater), I know that they have access to a trusted adult, and someone other than their parents is monitoring their attendance, behavior, and grades. This way, their academic and social-emotional well-being has a safety net. Most importantly, involvement deepens a student's sense of belonging to our school.

There is a lot of research that shows that students who participate in extracurricular activities have better attendance, grades, and behavior than students who do not participate. I share data from the National Center for Education Statistics (NCES) (1995) and the National Association of Secondary School Principals (NASSP) (2016) with parents and students by saying, "I can't ignore the plethora of data that shows you will have more success as a student if you get involved in one of our many student organizations."

In my secondary schools, I assigned an assistant principal to manage student activities. Honestly, I inherited this model, but I soon understood the value of it. There are many spinning wheels involved with student organizations: membership, schedules, activities, meetings, and even the purpose and function of that group. Here is a confession of why it is important to delegate student activities.

As a new principal, I started working at a school where the practice was for the theater teacher to secure the principal's approval before starting any theater productions. Prior to this, I honestly did not know that there were high school productions that were controversial or risqué. One time, I was in the hallway when the theater teacher stopped me to explain that she needed to change the production from The Little Orphan Annie *to what I understood to be* You're in Town. *She gave a very broad synopsis of the play, saying that it dealt*

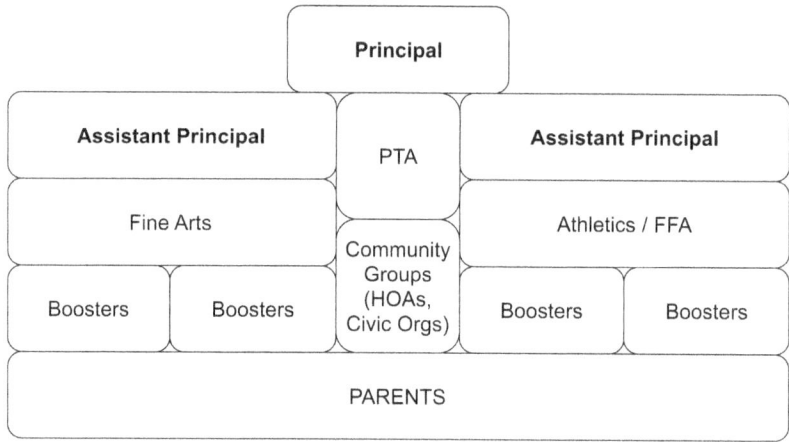

Figure 5.3 Parent-community organization.

with the scarcity of water. Without much thought, I approved and asked her to send me the dates of production so I could attend. Saying "yes" in moments like these made me feel good as a principal. I liked knowing that a teacher or student received the affirmation they were looking for or had an obstacle removed so they could accomplish their goal. But it only feels good until that decision, that approval, goes bad!

A few months later, close to opening night of You're in Town, *I heard announcements and saw posters for, to my surprise, shock, and horror,* Urinetown. *This play is indeed about the scarcity of water, but due to the scarcity, the citizens of Urinetown are charged to urinate or pee. WHAT? And I had also approved the elementary school's preview of our dress rehearsal. I raced to the theater teacher and expressed my frustration that she was not clearer in her explanation of this theater production. I demanded to see the full script immediately. I read through the script and found it to be a bit too edgy for our school community, but there was nothing I could do. We were just days away from opening night. I dropped everything to attend the remaining rehearsals, asked for a few edits that were allowable under the copyright agreement, and gritted my teeth as the play proceeded.*

As expected, I received complaints about the play being inappropriate for high school children. My favorite complaint was, "How did we go from Annie *to* Urinetown?" *Ultimately, I felt the production was good and appropriate, but had I understood why our theater teacher wanted to perform this play, I would have done more to prepare our community about the performance and why we chose it. This would have been a great time to practice the PROACTIVE communication that I knew the community needed. Nevertheless, after a few lumps, I got through it and instituted a new approval process for theatrical productions: "All productions must be submitted to the principal, with the full script and synopsis, at the beginning of the school year and approved by both an assistant principal and the principal." I wish I had delegated the theatre production to an AP earlier so that I would not have had to make an important decision in the hallway instead of giving it the attention it deserved.*

I recount that story to explain the importance of delegating student organizations so your administrative team can assist. Depending on the size of your school and how much attention is needed, you may want to assign two assistant principals, as depicted in the next chart. The one thing that I do not delegate is a Student Advisory group. If you don't have one, create one. This is a group of students who are informal leaders of your school. I recommend about five to ten students across various grade levels and subgroups of your student population. Meet with them regularly to learn more about what the students perceive as working and not working. Often, new ideas and policies will impact the student body. This is a good place to introduce those ideas so you can get feedback from a student's perspective.

The student structure is very similar to the parents, and if I had more than one AP for parents, I would assign the student organizations to the same assistant principal as the parent organizations (i.e., the band would be assigned to the same AP as the band boosters).

Ultimately, this provides a structure for your student groups (and the staff that lead or facilitate them) to have regular access to an administrator to accomplish the goals of their organization while abiding by the expectations, policies, and practices established for our campus (**Principal Presence**). They have someone to communicate with, and I have a way to ensure I know what is going on (**Principal Mystique**) and communicate my expectations.

Empower Your APs and Provide Principal Access

These structures are primarily for the purpose of communication. They enabled me to ensure everyone adhered to the goals and expectations I had for our school, and they provided consistency for whom students

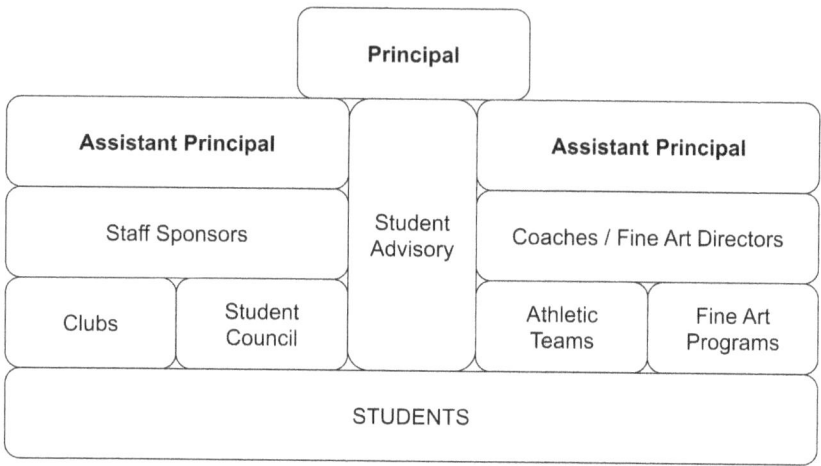

Figure 5.4 Student club organization.

and sponsors should contact when they needed assistance or approval (**Principal Presence**).

It is integral when developing the leadership skills of your assistant principals that you assign them a department, a few PLCs, and student and parent organizations. I would always explain to my APs that this department or PLC was their school within our school. They were the principal of these teachers and the students as it related to this department or student group. They were to lead, communicate, and engage with them as they would if they were the principal of that school. Empowering my APs allowed me to see them in action, especially their decision-making and ability to demonstrate **Principal Presence** and **Principal Mystique**. Don't expect the learning of leadership skills to be a one-way street. Over the years, I have learned from my APs too. There are many nuggets in this book that I learned or adapted from the wisdom and experiences of my APs.

Staff and students all understood that the APs and I met regularly, and they served as an extension of me. So, having an AP approve or disapprove something was equivalent to me doing so. Make no mistake, though— there were times when people appealed those decisions, or I voluntarily overturned them. But that is a part of growing and calibrating as a team. It is not a bad thing; it is growth.

These structures work both top down and bottom up. It really depends on the situation. It may not be popular to say or admit, but there are times when things need to be managed from the top down. In those cases, the reason should be clear. For example, requiring a standardized template for teacher collaboration (PLCs) or lesson plans should be a top-down expectation. However, establishing the template itself should be accomplished with input from staff, or bottom up.

Part II
How We
Do School

6 **Communication**

Communicate up, down and around. No one likes surprises!
DR. GOBER

I believe that an effective school principal should have five essential systems. Each system is managed from the top down and bottom up. I began teaching these five systems when I became a principal supervisor, and the principals I supervised called them the "Gober Five." They understood that every time I met with them, I wanted to see evidence and artifacts that demonstrated that these systems were implemented and monitored. Eventually, I was invited by the Texas Association of Secondary School Principals (TASSP) to present on this topic, and I have been presenting regularly for almost a decade. It is important to understand that as a principal supervisor and presenter to principals across my state, I constantly modify these systems. They are not "turnkey" or new; I merely explain practical ways to implement and monitor established best practices. Let's look at these systems, starting with communication.

Developing a system to provide timely and effective communication to all of the stakeholders of any school can be complex and overwhelming. Principals often do not think it through or plan it out thoroughly. So, let's slow down and think about who needs regular communication from the principal, the best vehicle to deliver that communication, and the optimum frequency. Let's not forget to build a system that efficiently allows stakeholders to communicate with you; failure to do this usually propels the principal into the role of a firefighter who constantly reacts to fires by answering emails, phone calls, and meeting requests from stakeholders.

Know Your Stakeholders

Most would agree that the primary stakeholders are your students, staff, parents, community, and district administration, including the school board. There are also secondary and tertiary stakeholders such as local businesses, realtors, alumni, teacher associations, your elected officials, and your state education department. I mostly focus on the primary stakeholders with the assumption that the secondary and tertiary stakeholders are among the "community."

Communication should flow in two directions. We will focus on what, how, and when the principal communicates to stakeholders and then look at how stakeholders can communicate with the principal.

Your primary stakeholders should be able to expect weekly communication from you. If you do less than that, stakeholders could perceive that you are not engaged, and people may not receive information in a timely fashion. If you do more, people tend to tune out and ignore your messages. I have found that communication once a week, on the same day and at the same time each week, to be most effective. This communication system has three prongs: communication with staff, communication with parents and community, and communication with students.

The Three-Pronged Plan for Communication

People love predictability when it comes to receiving communication! The staff and community knew that I would always send the staff and community communication on Monday at noon. Doing so prevented a lot of emails and phone inquiries from Tuesday through Sunday. (Well, maybe not Tuesday because if I forgot to include something on Monday, I was certain to hear about it by Tuesday.) The students knew they would hear from me every Friday morning during school announcements.

The Staff Monday Memo

Let's start with your staff. Traditionally, school leaders have held regular staff meetings to inform the staff of campus events, conduct required training, review data, and celebrate successes. Staff meetings are challenging to schedule due to the many activities and programs constantly going on, and they become almost impossible at secondary schools, which usually results in two meetings—one before school and one after school to accommodate the athletic coaches and club sponsors. Some principals have been creative and utilize the PLC time built into the schedule to travel through those teams throughout the day to ensure they meet with all staff, and still others utilize a daily or weekly "principal's memo," usually in the form of an email. Regardless of how or when it is done, one thing is certain—you need to meet with your staff because operating a school often calls for a lot of logistics, training, planning, and sharing of information.

The goal of any system is to be efficient and effective but also practical and sustainable. A combination of both in-person meetings and written memos allows for just that. The principal memo, what I call the "Monday Memo," should be weekly and serve as your portable staff meeting. Video conferencing and asynchronous video memos are becoming more popular, especially after Covid-19, but I have found that the electronic written memo is best for staff because of the ability to link documents, articles, and helpful websites for your staff. There are many vendors that offer products that make producing a professional memo easy, help you manage the mailing lists, and provide data on who opened it and clicked on certain links, and so on. Two examples are Constant Contact and Smore. I particularly like these types of products because they provide templates with the ability to add or embed a video or website link, share with other contributors, and create an archive of previous memos.

So, what goes into this Monday Memo? Staff will need to contribute some items. They can either submit them for you to cut and paste into your memo, or you can give contributors access to edit your memo. That decision is based on your own comfort level, but you must establish clear parameters about correct spelling, grammar, style, and format and create deadlines for submission. My deadline was Monday at 9:00 a.m. It was firm, and there were many times that people were frustrated with me because I rarely made an exception (which led to fewer future violations of the deadline).

I experimented with content every year I served as principal, and I will share what I found to be essential. I will also share what I learned to be great "bonus" material, along with a few ideas that went terribly wrong.

Essential content for the Monday Memo is anything that would have been communicated in most traditional staff meetings. Below are sections that I included, or have seen included, in Monday Memos. I identify the team or person responsible for contributing to that section in brackets [ ].

- **Message from the Principal**—Sometimes finding something to say is difficult, and sometimes it is tempting to say too much, but it is always important for your staff to hear from you. Continually establish your **Principal Presence**. Messages can be about infinite things: restating expectations, thanking the PTA, reviewing some data that you recently discovered, and giving praise and recognition for hard work or dedication are examples. This message should be one to two paragraphs and light and easy for staff to read. [Principal]

- **Reminders/Deadlines/Tasks**—You will inevitably need to remind staff about completing a task or meeting a deadline. [Principal and Admin Team]

- **Share Instructional Snapshot Data (The Snapshot Mirror)**—This reflects what instruction looks like at your school (explained more in Chapter 9, "Instructional Snapshots"). This section is an absolute necessity when you are implementing instructional snapshots. [Principal]

- **Spotlight Upcoming School Events**—This helps everyone engage with what is happening at the school and hopefully yields higher staff participation at events. I never expected staff to attend all school events, but I wanted them to know about them so they could use that information when working with students and forming relationships, thus enhancing their teacher **Mystique**. [Leadership Team, Coaches, Sponsors]

   A math teacher says to a student: "Sydney, I saw that our school team is going to the playoffs. I am so excited for you and the team."

   Science PLC conversation: "Let's ask the Theater teacher if she can provide us a few free tickets for the upcoming musical to use as incentives for those students who showed the most growth on our last assessment."

- **One-Stop Shopping**—Everyone appreciates a shortcut! Provide links to apps, tools, and websites that the staff use regularly. Examples include the school website, PTA website, data portal, curriculum planners, and district resources. [Admin Team]

- **Links to the School Calendar**—If you cannot embed a master calendar that shows all of the significant campus events, it certainly needs to be linked. It should already be on the school's web page. Both the calendar and campus website should be maintained and up-to-date. [Campus Webmaster]

- **Archive (Internally)**—You will want to archive and provide a link to the archives of previous Monday Memos to allow staff and sometimes yourself the ability to reference a previous memo.

- **Staff Highlights**—This special section is especially useful for a large staff, as it allows everyone to learn more about fellow staff members each week. It's a great morale booster and often quite informative. It also allows you, the principal, to know your staff better, thus enhancing your **Principal Mystique**. [I assigned to an AP]

- **Link to Anonymously Communicate to the Principal**—I used a Google Form where the "Collect Email Addresses" setting was turned off. You may think this could open Pandora's box, and I cannot guarantee that it never will, but I can tell you that I was able to learn *a lot*. It was like steroids for my **Principal Mystique**. Having the ability to share something with the principal without fear of anyone knowing who it came from allows staff to share many nuggets about the campus, staff, and students that you would not have known otherwise. I did have a caveat that I would not respond because I wouldn't know who to respond to. Over time, I added a section in the memo called "Ask Dr. G." Staff could submit questions anonymously, and the next week I would write the question and my response for the whole staff to see. Again, no one knew where the question came from, but if I felt it was beneficial for the whole staff to know my response, I would share it there. This became one of the most popular features of my Monday Memo.

Bonus content is not essential, but I have found that staff really enjoy these sections:

- **Highlight Best Practices**—A very popular feature in a memo was "Caught Ya Teaching." This was a short video clip (from a phone camera) embedded in the memo that showed the greatness of a teacher or class. A word of caution: if you start this, be careful not to commit to it every week. There are some weeks where you don't "catch" greatness in the classroom. This is not to say that it did not exist, just that you did not capture it. [Admin Team and Instructional Coaches]

- **Links to Professional Learning Articles/TED Talks**—Staff really enjoy short articles and videos that inform on best practices, self-care, or genuinely interesting topics. I encouraged the staff to be lifelong learners, and I found that when I made it easy to access learning, many consumed it. [Librarian/Media Specialist and Instructional Coaches (ICs)]

- **Humorous/Interesting Videos**—These can be less about learning and just humorous or entertaining. A clever meme or newspaper cartoon is always fun, especially if it is about teaching or school. One week, I included a link to the zoo that had a live feed on the chimpanzees. The staff loved it! [Librarian and ICs]

- **Contests**—I started this before I had the ability to know who opened my memo, but I kept doing it from time to time because the staff loved it. Examples: creating a treasure hunt with weekly clues only found in the Monday Memo. During Thanksgiving, it might read, "Turkey Contest: I have free turkeys for the first three people to meet me at the one place in our building where taking drugs is appropriate." [Admin Team]

- **Staff Recipes**—I reluctantly agreed to this, and little did I know that the staff had a treasure of great recipes. This feature turned into an unenforced requirement that everyone try that recipe that week. Many staff members loved it because it provided them with ideas for that night's dinner. [Librarian]

- **Staff Family Highlights**—Highlighting staff is essential, but they also love it when you highlight their family. They are dying to share photos of grandchildren, recall a story about their vacation, or beam with pride over a video of their cat. By the way, you can learn from me, or you will learn the hard way, that you have to set parameters such as no more than two paragraphs, thirty-second videos, and/or two photos. [assigned to an AP]

- **Monthly Department Features**—I had a "counselor's corner" that turned into a weekly feature where the counselors gave tips on social-emotional learning (SEL), how to write recommendation letters, tips for studying, how to conduct an effective parent-teacher conference, and other useful information. You can offer it weekly, monthly, or whatever frequency is most appropriate for your school. [Specific Departments, Counselors, Nurse, Librarian]

Everything needs to be done with discretion. For example, if you are only including the same two people's recipes, you will hear complaints unless you truly have someone with the talent of Martha Stewart. Do not add a political cartoon, meme, or video that is too controversial or not appropriate for school. Do not use the principal's message every week to bark directives and expectations—you need to be balanced.

Steer clear of favoritism. Be careful about what is written and how often you write about a person or group in staff highlights or recognitions; this is why I delegate this section. Too much praise for the football team alienates the other coaches. You already highlighted that awesome science teacher, and everyone knows how great she is. Surely you can find someone else doing great things.

Pay attention to the anonymous communication. Be mindful that if a staff member shares something that is a concern, they share it with the expectation that you will look into it and hopefully resolve the issue. I often received messages of a tattling nature: "I hope someone can talk to Ms. Rush about leaving early every day" or "I don't want to tattle, but I am not sure it is safe that Coach Sweat is having his team run in the extreme heat." This is all good information to know, but the report comes with the unspoken expectation that you do something about it.

As with every system highlighted here, you must be clear, consistent, and practical with your Monday Memo. It will not be sustainable if you make it too involved, requiring hours of maintenance each week. It will also lose its value and purpose if it does not have relevance to the staff. It will take some trial and error, but you will find the sweet spot to ensure this is a sustainable tool in your communication system with staff.

The School Newsletter (Parents and Community)

The second prong of our three-prong communication system is a tool for parent communication. Let's not forget that parents and the community require proactive, relevant, and timely communication. For those looking for a shortcut, there is a bit of one here: some of the sections in your staff Monday Memo can be used for your School Newsletter. So, depending on your format, you can either copy or duplicate your staff memo, removing those links and sections that are not relevant or appropriate for anyone other than staff and adding a few more sections.

You absolutely must keep the "Principal's Message" section. The message may need to change, but this is your opportunity to share your vision, mission, goals, and expectations with your parents. You can maintain your **Principal Presence** as well as enhance your **Principal Mystique** by sharing information about the various things you know. In the first newsletter of the year (and I would recommend reiterating for the first four weeks or so), explain the function and dynamics of the newsletter.

I have subscribed all of our parents to receive our weekly newsletter, which comes from my desk to your email every Monday at 12:00 p.m. This newsletter will only be sent to you once a week, and I encourage you to peruse it to stay informed about the "happenings" at the high school. In each newsletter, you will find links to important websites or documents and our up-to-date school calendar, which lists every event held on our campus. You will also find highlights of our students and updates on our clubs, fine arts programs, and athletic teams. Please note that I do not personally provide all of the information for these updates. I rely on our coaches, directors, or sponsors to provide the content to me each week before I send it out each Monday at noon. You can quickly navigate our newsletter with the bookmarks provided in the right margin that will take you to the content of your choice.

Of course, I would also say, "Welcome back to school!" and give some reminders, but it is important that you train your parents to look for this newsletter each week.

Over time, I had to remind parents about various things in my principal message. For example, "Please don't expect to hear baseball news during football season or updates on the marching band during the spring," and "Please help me by working with your coach or director to ensure their updates are accurate and submitted on time each week."

This School Newsletter doubles as community communication. If you are using a subscription-based tool, anyone can subscribe or unsubscribe at will. Don't forget that your school website should have a link to your newsletter and archives with information on how to subscribe. I also recommend subscribing your principal supervisor, superintendent, and school board members to your newsletter.

The content here is similar to the staff newsletter. You need essential information that is always included, and over time, you will add to this or have a monthly feature.

- **Message from the Principal**—Always communicate your priorities and high expectations for students and staff. Share opportunities for parents to get involved and interesting facts about the school. And always convey your pride in being the principal. I would always sign my letters and this section of the newsletter like this: *With [Mascot] pride, Dr. Courtney Gober.* (With Wolverine Pride, With Tiger Pride, With Eagle Pride, etc.) [Principal]
- **Reminders/Deadlines/Tasks**—You will need to remind parents to turn in permission slips or submit absence notes, as well as encourage them to buy a yearbook or sign up for PTA. [Admin Team]
- **Spotlight Upcoming School Events**—Encourage participation and support for all school events. If nothing else, it keeps everyone informed. If you subscribed your school board members and they see your parking lot full on a Saturday night, they won't email you to ask what's going on. [Leadership Team, Coaches, Sponsors]
- **One-Stop Shopping**—Everyone appreciates a shortcut! Provide links to commonly used apps, tools, and websites that parents regularly use. Examples: school website, PTA website, lunch accounts, district website, and adult/parent education opportunities in the district or community. [Leadership Team]
- **Student ACADEMIC-ONLY Highlights**—The only highlights outside of student groups or teams were clearly distinguishable individual academic highlights. Athletes and others were highlighted in a later section. Examples: perfect ACT scores, National Merit Finalists, and students with perfect attendance [Leadership Team]
- **Athletic/Fine Arts/Extracurricular Highlights**—This was a huge favorite and was exclusively fed by the coaches and sponsors of the student groups. I did have to give some parameters about not bashing other schools to prevent the football coach from saying something like, "Come on out on Friday as we take on the Eagles and turn them into Chickens!" [Coaches and Sponsors]
- **Links to the School Calendar**—If you cannot embed your master calendar that shows all of the significant campus events, it certainly needs to be linked. It should already be on the school's web page. Both the calendar and campus website should be maintained and up-to-date. [Campus Webmaster]

- **Archive (Internally)**—You will want to archive and provide a link to the archives to allow references to previous newsletters.
- **Link to Anonymously Communicate to the Principal**—Again, be mindful that when someone shares a concern, they expect that it will be looked into and hopefully resolved. These messages were often "tips," and we later created a tip line because I wanted to ensure that multiple people received the tip in case it was time-sensitive or a true emergency to school safety or security. Don't forget to have a note in your anonymous form that explains you will not respond unless they leave their email address because this form does not require you to input an email address. [Principal]

Bonus content that parents really enjoyed in the past:

- **Staff Highlights**—This is a special section that allows everyone to learn more about our staff each week. [APs]
- **Humorous/Interesting Videos**—Sometimes, we included clever memes, videos, or newspaper cartoons that were 100 percent appropriate with topics relating to parenting, school, or a noncontroversial social issue. Example: a cartoon depicting the "Longest Spring Break Ever" referencing the beginning of Covid-19 in 2020. [Librarian]
- **Department Features**: This included the Counselor's Corner, From the Nurse Clinic, Technology Tips for Parents, and so on. [Leadership Team and Others]
- **Understanding School Language**—This turned out to be a favorite for parents. We started by explaining social-emotional learning (SEL), and then we taught about other acronyms used in school. [ICs and Counselors]
- **How-to**—This proved to be a great tool, even though the staff thought it was going to be disastrous. In this section, we would explain the process for disputing a grade, requesting a schedule change, filing a complaint or appeal, the difference between bullying and being mean, and so on. We also provided links to relevant documents or websites on these topics. [Admin Team]
- **PTA and Booster Clubs**—I allowed short announcements and highlights from these groups. [PTA and Booster Clubs]

As with the Monday Memo, everything needs to be done with discretion. I would be careful about what is written and how often you write about a person or group in highlights or recognitions. Too much praise for the football team alienates the band parents. Also, unless you have a very small school, don't include individual student birthdays! It is a never-ending, hot mess of complaints because someone's birthday will be left off, or someone will not be recognized.

Remember, your newsletter needs to be clear, consistent, and practical. Keep it simple so that it is sustainable. Lastly, keep it relevant so it does not lose its value and purpose. This tool will become a treasure for your school. Over time, if you are consistent, you will notice fewer inquiries in your email, and your parents and community will become more informed about your school. And two last tips that are too important to overlook: First, everyone who contributes to the newsletter needs to understand that you are the final editor. You will edit as you deem necessary or appropriate, often without notifying the contributor of the edit. They need to know this up front, or they will complain once they see that you changed something. Second, never send the newsletter (or Monday Memo) out twice, even if there is a mistake (unless it is an absolutely critical mistake). Using a subscription service like Constant Contact or Smore will help avoid this temptation to resend because they allow you to edit and republish while maintaining the link that you've already sent out. The importance of ensuring accurate information cannot be overstated. Have your secretary, or whoever has a reputation in your front office for details, proofread all dates and times for accuracy.

Communication with Students

I am appalled at how many times I have visited campuses and asked students, "Who is your principal?" only to be met with, "I don't know," or the student incorrectly named an assistant principal or counselor. Everyone should know who the principal is—every student, staff, and parent. For a student not to know who the principal is sends a red flag that the principal is disengaged and clearly lacks **Principal Presence**.

Weekly communication with your students is paramount for you to be able to set expectations, influence student and staff morale, and model the character traits of a [insert your mascot]. *Every student should know the principal by name, face, and established expectations.*

The most effective tool for student communication is your morning announcements, followed by every school assembly, pep rally, and ceremony. In several schools, our morning announcements were produced daily in our Audio/Video room. Mimicking a nightly newscast, we had two anchors, a sports reporter, and Gober Facetime on Fridays (**Principal Presence**). My two- to three-minute segment was my opportunity to let the students know more about me: my vision and goals for the school, expectations for behavior, beliefs about the classroom being sacred for learning, and, of course, more about me as a person and trusted adult. I would celebrate team wins, pump everyone up to go to the game, and use my **Principal Mystique** and sense of humor to assure them that I knew everything.

> *Our biology students are dissecting pigs this week; therefore, the cafeteria will be selling extra bacon for one week only.*
>
> *It's prom season, so if you need dating advice, I am sure Coach [insert name of coach who is not likely to give advice and does not mind your teasing] won't mind helping you out.*
>
> *It is getting cold outside, and I know it is cold in the building—no, we don't wear pajamas to school, and no, we don't wear hoodies on our head. Let Dr. G help you with advice on how to layer. First, start with lotion, then an undershirt, then a polo shirt with a nice sweater on top. Not only will you be warm, your skin won't be ashy or dry.*

Yes, show your personality. Have fun! You are in the kid business. Your years of teaching and AP experience have allowed you to master the art of meeting kids at their level. Show the staff that you are a relationship builder. Show your students that you are an approachable principal with high expectations for learning and behavior who is proud to be their principal.

I also used Gober Facetime to enforce some staff expectations. For example, during state testing week, I told the staff that no one was to give homework, make an assignment due, or give a test. I did not want to go around checking to see if they were following my directive, so I told the students, "Next week, we have state testing. I know you are prepared and ready to show your brilliance, and therefore, there will not be any homework or tests given next week. I want you well rested and in top form, so I've spoken with all your teachers about making sure they don't assign any homework or tests for next week." Now, do you really think a teacher would try to give homework? Well, yes . . . there's always that English teacher who only assigned a few pages of reading or the history teacher who thinks he is a Harvard professor. Don't worry—before the end of second period, you will have at least three students inform you of this heinous crime. Also, don't forget that you have anonymous reporting tools for staff, parents, and students.

Yes, students need to be able to talk to the principal anonymously. I had a tip line for safety and security reporting, but I also created both a Google Form and a good old-fashioned locked box where they could drop a note. Of course, I had to explain how to use the "Gober Box" (**Principal Presence**) and that emergencies should be reported by using the tip line or going directly to an adult, but oh, what glorious information I gleaned from the students! It was benign information about their lunch menu preferences, which teachers they liked and disliked, and their opinions about the tardy procedures and makeup work policy. I got it all, including rumors, gossip, and an occasional inappropriate comment or complaint. But all of it was information that I quietly absorbed and used to help me with decision-making and planning (**Principal Mystique**). Over time, anonymous access to you will become one of your most valuable tools.

Other things I employed with Gober Facetime were hallway pep rallies: "Teachers, please open your doors and let me hear the third-floor shout [insert school chant] 1, 2, 3 [insert school chant]. Alright, second-floor students, I know you can do better than that. 1, 2, 3 [insert school chant]." You are the principal, the key influencer of school culture and morale. Don't delegate this responsibility, and do not make light of it. Use your **Principal Presence** and **Principal Mystique** to win your students over. Let it never be said that a student in your school does not know who the principal is.

7 Collaboration

Why do we need staff meetings when we have the Monday Memo and PLC time?
DR. GOBER

Collaborate or Co-blaborate

Effective collaboration absolutely cannot and will not happen without the principal's devoted effort and enthusiasm to ensure that a collaborative culture exists. Creating that culture will most likely involve direct leadership and invoking your **Principal Presence**.

I recall interviewing for a principal position where the committee, made up of district and community leaders, asked the typical questions but focused heavily on my knowledge of Professional Learning Communities (PLCs). Recognizing the importance of PLCs to the district, I shifted my responses from discussing my knowledge to emphasizing my ability to implement and monitor them. After I was hired, I was told the campus had already begun PLC implementation, as reflected in the master schedule. When I inquired about templates and monitoring processes, I was informed that each PLC created its own template and that campus administrators were assigned to oversee them.

After asking for the existing PLC templates, I received over twenty variations after two weeks, with only a handful aligning with Dufour's (2006) four essential PLC questions:

1. What is it we want our students to know and be able to do?
2. How will we know if each student has learned it?
3. How will we respond when some students do not learn it?
4. How will we extend the learning for students who have demonstrated proficiency?

It became clear that while the campus had some PLC training, the structure and implementation were inconsistent. District leaders had referenced the campus as a model of PLC implementation, which left me second-guessing my understanding. I went back to studying PLC resources and eventually realized that we were missing critical elements.

I began reteaching my assistant principals and instructional coaches, who embraced the changes and sought guidance on how to improve. However, when I introduced these ideas to department chairs, I encountered some resistance. The teachers believed they were already doing effective work and saw PLCs as a formal recognition of their existing team meetings. They were satisfied with having common planning periods built into the schedule, a long-demanded change, and they didn't fully grasp the distinction between regular team meetings and true PLCs.

Reflecting on my observations at hundreds of different campuses, I've noticed that many schools claim to have implemented PLCs simply because they allocate meeting time. However, they often lack a deeper focus on Dufour's essential questions and fail to monitor PLC effectiveness. In reality, many teachers are engaged in what Dufour calls "co-blaboration" (2016, p. 59). Teachers are collaborating but are not focused on the right work.

Good Is the Enemy of Great

The world-renowned author and teacher of leaders Jim Collins states,

> *Good is the enemy of great. And that is one of the key reasons why we have so little that becomes great. We don't have great schools, principally because we have good schools. We don't have great government, principally because we have good government. Few people attain great lives, in large part because it is just so easy to settle for a good life. (Collins, 2001)*

I became the new principal at a "good" campus, which I welcomed after leaving a school with shifting demographics and unstable district leadership. The previous environment had made it difficult to implement systems for campus stability and early interventions for students in need.

The temptation to maintain the status quo and avoid the challenges of correcting PLC misinterpretations is common, especially when a school is functioning well and staff are happy. It's easy to let teachers continue to use existing templates that may only reflect agendas, not true collaboration or data-driven planning. However, real leadership requires resisting the urge to settle for "good" and instead striving for "great."

To move forward, instructional leaders must have the courage and confidence to implement true Professional Learning Communities with fidelity, even if it means facing resistance from staff. This includes holding every team accountable to using a consistent PLC template that requires reviewing data, planning effective instruction, and addressing gaps in student learning. To create **Principal Presence** and add to your **Principal Mystique**, you must consistently monitor these processes, providing support and feedback to ensure that collaborative work stays focused on improving student outcomes.

It's also critical to review end-of-year data, not only to celebrate successes but also to identify gaps, particularly for marginalized student groups. Every educator should be committed to closing achievement gaps and ensuring that all students, regardless of background, show academic growth. Summer is an ideal time to reset and communicate these expectations: weekly PLC meetings, use of a unified template, administrative presence and feedback, and focused discussions around key instructional questions. Establishing systems that utilize Google Forms and Google Sheets for monitoring progress ensures both accountability and practicality for staff.

True greatness, as Jim Collins reminds us, is a conscious choice, not a function of circumstance. Leaders must push beyond comfort to create systems that drive student success, even when it's difficult.

Figure 7.1 is one of my favorite PLC templates.

Administrators in PLCs

"How will we know if all of this is making a difference?" This question from both DuFour et al. (2006) and my teachers haunted me throughout our PLC implementation. I decided to measure success by the growth and achievement of our most vulnerable students, emphasizing that our greatness would now be defined by closing achievement gaps. With support from the district and input from teachers, we set specific goals for each PLC aimed at improving outcomes for students who traditionally struggled.

To support this, I assigned assistant principals and instructional coaches to monitor and attend weekly PLC meetings. Whether they could attend or not, they were required to review the PLC's work, provide feedback, and remove obstacles that hindered progress. Administrators were tasked with regularly

Professional Learning Community Agenda

Algebra 1 Team	Campus Expectations and Norms	
Date: Members Present: 6th period / Room 201	1. Meet at least once per week. 2. Use PLC Google Template (Share with Principal, AP, and IC) 3. Everyone participates and all voices are heard. 4. Come prepared (take care of personal needs before or after) 5. Be productive. Stay focused on the planning and the agenda. 6. Be solution oriented.	
Data Used Today	**Data Celebrations (2 min)**	
Formative Assessments • Bell Ringer • Exit Ticket • Other Summative Assessments • Unit Test • State Test • PSAT/SAT/ACT • Other	1. 2. 3. 4. 5.	
Essential Questions	**Plan**	**Reference**
What do want students to learn?		(Standards/Objectives)
How do we know students have learned?		(Data used)
How do we differentiate for students who learn quickly?		(MTSS-Acceleration)
How do we differentiate for students who learn slowly?		(MTSS-Intervention)
Student Engagement	(Plan and Evidence)	
Team Notes	(Action Items with person assigned. Follow ups / Questions)	
Goals for Next Meeting	(Goal(s), date and materials to bring. Who is responsible for what?)	
Instructional Leadership	(What is needed from campus or district administration?)	

Figure 7.1 Sample PLC template.

visiting classrooms, conducting "snapshots," and sharing successes in our communications. I empowered my team to act as leaders of their "school within a school," guiding, supporting, and making decisions for their group of teachers. This approach fostered a sense of ownership (though, at times, I had to balance their leadership zeal with giving teachers the space they needed).

A True PLC Culture

You are the principal. You are a key influencer of the culture at this campus. I truly believe this. One of my mantras is that the classroom is sacred; another is that PLC time is sacred. Finding ways to add time to PLCs, reduce distractions, and remove obstacles is a constant chore for a principal. Often, people are tempted to use that time to accomplish an administrative task, but you must remain committed to ensuring that PLC time is built into the schedule each year. As time passes, you may be able to squeeze even more minutes into that time.

I wanted a campus culture that did not just say it was a PLC campus. I wanted it to be so evident that it did not have to be said—it was just known that *this is how we do school*. I never wanted PLCs to be seen as "something else" or an added task for our teachers. We needed to establish them as a foundational requisite for teaching. Over time, our students began to understand what PLCs were and that if a group of teachers were in collaboration or PLC time, they were treated as students taking a state test—do not disturb. Receiving district accolades or even recognition was never my goal. However, I admit that I felt accomplished when a parent asked the English teachers to consider something specific the next time they were in their PLC. Even the parents knew that PLCs were where the magic happened.

If PLCs were *how we do school*, then what about lesson planning and a Multi-Tiered System of Support (MTSS)? Teachers who plan and prepare using relevant formative and summative data are not doing anything extra; they are doing the work that is necessary to calibrate the delivery of their instruction. PLCs provide the foundation to create effective lesson plans, and PLCs are the vehicle for academic monitoring and planning the interventions needed for MTSS.

8 Lesson Planning

A teacher without a lesson plan is like a principal without systems.
DR. GOBER

"Lesson planning" may be bad words, depending on where you are and what is expected in your plan. I understand this as well as the recent legal arguments that requiring lesson plans may violate the Paperwork Reduction Act (Legal Digest, 2015). However, we cannot ignore the true purpose of lesson plans or the power of lesson plans as roadmaps for reaching learning objectives.

Nothing New

Do not get caught up in fads. Learn best practices and what makes sense for you to implement on your campus. I vehemently argue that lesson plans are not a fad or added paperwork—they are a necessity! There is nothing remarkably new in teaching; there are only new ways to look at things and better tools available for educators and schools. A major obstacle to schools finding success is a principal losing sight of fundamental best practices. Establishing what students need to learn (learning objectives) and designing the instruction to accomplish those objectives are at the foundation of the teaching profession.

Implementing PLCs builds a natural bridge for lesson planning. Most of the "work" in planning lessons is usually accomplished in the PLC. We need to document what, when, and how lessons get taught. I have gone through many renditions of lesson plan templates in my career, and I have concluded that there is no panacea for planning or a magic template for me to promote. Ultimately, what is expected in a lesson should be decided in collaboration with your campus leaders and teachers. Here is another opportunity to invest in a technology tool. There are at least a dozen companies that have simplified lesson plans to a series of mouse clicks and a few lines of text.

Lesson planning is not as laborious as it once was, and after creating lesson plans for one year, subsequent years become even less burdensome because teachers can update and modify existing lesson plans based on their notes and data from PLCs.

Wiggins and McTighe's *Understanding by Design* (1998) accurately reflects my expectations in lesson planning. Their work does not prescribe a model or template to use, but their concept of backward design is paramount to the success of lesson planning today. Understanding what is assessed and how it is assessed is the anchor to developing the learning objectives and activities required in the lesson plan. My nonnegotiables for lesson planning consisted of the following:

1. A common campus template that is teacher-friendly, which must at minimum consist of:
   - A learning objective
   - A brief description of the daily learning activities that were aligned to the assessment(s)
   - Copies or links to the formative and summative assessments
2. Space built in for administrative feedback on the lesson.

Let's take a look at a sample template in Figure 8.1.

This sample template should only take about thirty minutes to complete using Google Forms and Google Sheets that have drop-down lists and "clickable" boxes to check. Again, there are much more advanced and specialized technology tools available for purchase that are extremely teacher-friendly, which reduces the time required to create the plan.

Lesson Plan Essentials—The Heading

Let's examine what I expected more closely. The heading consisted of the obligatory date, title, name of course, and teacher. The textbook should not be the only thing listed under "Materials" each day. It can be listed, but what other resources are being used to provide an engaging, relevant, and optimal learning experience for our students? Then, the state objectives to cover, or "uncover," as Wiggins and McTighe aptly state, need to be listed.

Lesson Planning				
Course / Teacher(s)	**Lesson Title**			
State Learning Objective(s)	**Materials** (with links to documents)			
[Create drop down menu of objectives with "Priority" objectives bolded]				
	Learning Activity			**Assessments** (links to assessments)
Monday	(Learning Objective) Brief Description			
Tuesday	(Learning Objective) Brief Description			
Wednesday	(Learning Objective) Brief Description			
Thursday	(Learning Objective) Brief Description			
Friday	(Learning Objective) Brief Description			
[insert a drop-down menu or clickable items]	**Thinking Level**	**Type of Assessments Used**	**Instructional Strategies Used**	**Learning Environment**
Modifications and Extensions	[insert common items as a drop-down menu or a clickable item]			
Intervention Strategies for Targeted Students	[insert evidence-based strategies as a drop-down menu or a clickable item]			
Instructional Leadership Feedback				

Figure 8.1 Sample lesson planning template.

Let's discuss these state learning objectives. First, whether you are using Google or technology purchased through a vendor, these objectives can be added to the template at the beginning of the year so that they only require the click of a drop-down or a check in a box. Next, using your data tools, you can determine which state objectives are a "priority" on district and state assessments. Priority objectives that have been identified as most essential to a particular grade level, content area, or course need to be treated as a priority in lesson planning. Finally, encourage your PLCs to monitor and track how often each state objective is taught. Most of the new technology tools for lesson planning and data analysis come with this type of reporting feature. This is crucial when troubleshooting or trying to find the root cause for unsuccessful learning or growth.

Lesson Plan Essentials—Learning Activities

I have always thought that finding the learning activities was the most difficult part of lesson planning. Ideally, every day should have an activity that engages students with higher-order thinking, collaboration, and opportunities for differentiation. Lessons should be engaging, relevant, and aligned to the learning objective. This is the goal, but it will take time to get there.

I always taught my teachers the Backward Design Model, which means starting with how the learning objectives were to be assessed. Knowing how learning objectives are assessed is paramount to designing the learning activities; it is possible to teach a learning objective with formative assessments showing that students have mastered it only to have most of your students fail to meet that same learning objective on the district or state assessment.

Sample Fourth-grade Math Lesson

Let's look at a sample fourth-grade math learning objective: *the student is expected to identify right, acute, and obtuse angles*. First, the teacher designed a learning activity that had students learn the definitions of the angles (see Figure 8.2).

Next, the teacher had the students trace various iterations of the different angles.

And finally, the teacher gave an exit ticket that further met the learning objective: "The student is expected to *identify* right, acute, and obtuse angles."

This is great! It was fully aligned to the objective, and students did well on the formative assessment. The teacher felt accomplished, and the students

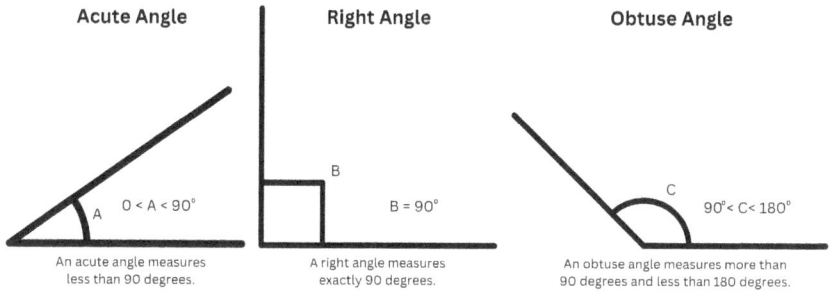

Figure 8.2 Definitions of angles.

felt confident in their knowledge of angles. Then, the students were exposed to the same learning objective as it was measured on the state assessment, which looked like that in Figure 8.4.

Now, most of the students may have been able to transfer their learning to an object that contains multiple angles. But all of their exposure with this learning objective was to single graphics in isolation from any other distractor. No one will argue that the teacher had a good lesson, taught the objective, gave them practice, and assessed their learning. She covered the learning objective. However, she did not teach or assess the learning objective the way the state measured it, which took the simple objective of "identifying" and made it relevant to real-life objects. She did not "uncover" this learning objective.

Lesson Plan Essentials—Feedback

In the example lesson plan, there are check boxes for Levels of Thinking, Type of Assessment, Instructional Strategies, Learning Environment, and two areas for teachers to write out differentiation strategies for extensions, modifications, or interventions. None of these items are essential, especially if they are already addressed in PLCs. However, the one area that is essential and shows **Principal Presence** is Instructional Leadership Feedback.

Part of closing the lesson plan loop is reviewing the lesson plans that you require your teachers to submit. If they are important enough to require teachers to do them, then they must be important enough for you to review. Reviewing lesson plans allows your teachers to see you in the trenches with them, and praising their planning goes a long way. The acclaimed scholar of

Write "A" if the angle is acute, "O" if it is obtuse, or "R" if it is right.

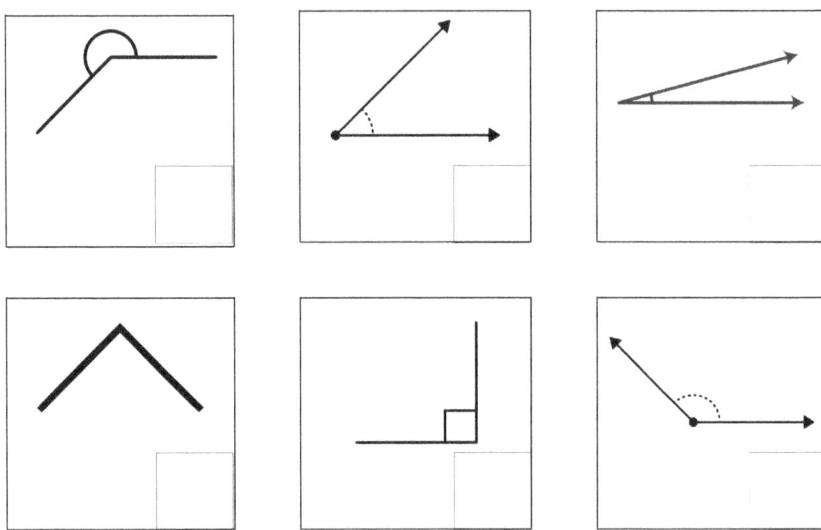

Figure 8.3 Exit ticket—angles.

leadership and management, Peter Drucker, said, "What gets measured gets done." To be clear, most campuses are large enough that the principal cannot provide feedback to all of the teachers each week. You must require your APs and other instructional leaders to share the load.

If I needed to be critical about lesson plans, my criticism usually fell in the area of alignment. When I asked my teachers to align their learning activities to the state objective, I implied that they should align the plan to *what* the learning objective measured and *how* it was measured. Moreover, I wanted to see that learning activities were engaging and *relevant*. Using the earlier grade four Math example, I would write my feedback as follows:

> *Consider adding the use of manipulatives, perhaps find a short video clip, or have students more active by having them make and identify angles with their arms to each other. Also, when reviewing item 13 on the state assessment, I am not seeing alignment in your learning activities to the way this objective is assessed. I have linked a few activities for you to consider for better alignment.*

Teekayu drew a cat's head shown below:

Which part of the cat's head appears to have acute angles?

A Eyes

B Nose

C Mouth

D Ears

Figure 8.4 State assessment question—angles.

Ultimately, this lesson plan lacked engagement and relevance, and it did not align with the way the learning objective was assessed. Following my feedback, I would expect to see some added engagement activities and an assessment that aligned with how the state was assessing this objective. Figure 8.5 is an example.

Identify the angle in each real-life object as acute, right, or obtuse.

Figure 8.5 Formative assessment—angles.

Further campus expectations for lesson planning were that:

- Everyone submitted lesson plans using the campus template.
- Plans were submitted weekly on Thursdays by 4:00 p.m. via Google.
- Instructional leaders (AP or IC) provided feedback by 4:00 p.m. on Fridays.
- Corrections from teachers were completed by 4:00 p.m. on Mondays.

As I mentioned earlier, share the responsibility of providing feedback with your leadership team. Assistant principals and other instructional leaders need to pitch in and divide this work for it to be manageable and sustainable. By requiring lesson plans to be submitted on Thursdays, I committed to providing feedback within twenty-four hours to ensure the plans would be updated for the following week. It took time, but I built this time into my schedule and required my administrators to do the same.

Lesson planning is too important for the principal and other instructional leaders to not be a part of it. I feel so strongly about this that I would further assert that if you cannot commit to providing feedback on lesson plans each week, then do not require them at all. If a campus does not already have an established culture of lesson planning, and you come in and require it, you will be met with resistance or menial compliance at first. Get in there with your teachers and assert your role as the principal-teacher. Show them how you earned your leadership role and, more importantly, show them the importance of lesson planning.

This system is difficult and takes time and discipline, especially for the first couple of years of implementation. But this system is where you can quickly maneuver school improvement levers. By reading and reviewing lesson plans, you will learn more about your teachers and the overall instructional capabilities of your staff. Lesson planning for teachers gets easier every year because the lessons are recycled with updates and upgrades. And since the lessons are recycled and updated, giving feedback becomes easier and eventually turns into genuine praise with the occasional reminder for a new teacher.

When I first started providing lesson plan feedback for the fifteen to twenty teachers in the Social Studies Department, it took me three to four hours each week. It did not take me long to realize that I needed to allow teachers of the same subject and in the same PLC to coauthor the plans. I also decided to limit my feedback to a specific theme for each grading period—for example, alignment, use of inquiry, or technology integration. With these modifications, reviewing and providing feedback was cut down from fifteen to twenty plans to about eight and from a few hours down to about ninety minutes each week.

I can recall discussing a lesson with an AP at a Friday night football game on more than one occasion. Great leadership training can come from this, especially when there is a difference of opinion on a lesson plan. Create a culture of learning, planning, communicating, and sharing. Make it appropriate, commonplace, and expected to discuss data, lesson plans, and intervention strategies with your staff. You are the principal—you set the tone!

9 **Instructional Snapshots**

Standing in front of the high school staff at the beginning of the school year, I explained what I had learned from Bob Marzano and Phil Warrick and my desire to be a High Reliability School. I asked the staff, "What does instruction look like in our school?"

DR. GOBER

High Reliability Schools

In all my years as an educator, there has never been a book or professional development more powerful to me and my development as an educational leader than *Leading a High Reliability School* (Marzano et al., 2018). The High Reliability School (HRS) model delineates twenty-five leading indicators organized into five levels (p. 30). Implementing these indicators can ultimately lead to becoming a high reliability school. After I read the book, Dr. Phil Warrick provided ongoing professional development, explaining each level and indicator with practical examples and strategies that were easy to employ.

I was sold! I absolutely believed in their research and believed it was best for students. The first three levels of the HRS Model were establishing a Safe, Supportive and Collaborative Culture (Level 1), ensuring Effective Teaching in Every Classroom (Level 2), and working with my district to provide a Guaranteed and Viable Curriculum (Level 3). I had complete principal autonomy over the first two levels, and I knew we could achieve them. The remaining three levels required the district to lead, and other than creating a Guaranteed and Viable Curriculum (Level 3), I was uncertain how committed the district was to developing Standards-Referenced Reporting (Level 4) and implementing a Competency-Based Education (Level 5).

Remember, you can only control what you've been given the autonomy to control. There was no time to pout about my inability to implement all five levels of HRS. The first two levels provided enough fodder to keep me focused and quite busy for a few years.

HRS Level 2—Effective Teaching in Every Classroom

The first indicator of HRS Level 2 profoundly changed me as a principal. It reads: "2.1—The school communicates a clear vision as to how teachers should address instruction" (p.77).

I quickly flashed back to all of the meetings and trainings I had with teachers, explaining teaching strategies and citing best practices as revealed in *The Fundamental Five* (Cain and Laird, 2011), *Teach Like a Champion* (Lemov, 2010), *What Great Teachers Do Differently* (Whitaker, 2012), and *The New Art and Science of Teaching* (Marzano, 2017) to name a few. I knew I communicated high expectations and had a system and process for most tasks, but I had never clearly communicated my instructional expectations for every teacher, every day, and in every classroom.

Only after talking to other principals and Dr. Warrick did I realize that it is common (shamefully) for schools to lack a clear vision, common language, and model of instruction. Whew.

But how could I have overlooked this? Easily. When it came to instructional expectations, I did what I saw others doing, and I did what principals before me had done—I unknowingly relied on hope. I was hoping that my teachers understood and were implementing *my unclear expectations* for effective instruction in every classroom. I recall a district leader sharing with principals that "hope is not a strategy for school improvement."

Instructional Model

I quickly consulted my leadership team. We developed a one-pager that clearly delineated our instructional model. The computer graphic design teacher took that document and transformed it into an attractive poster.

Then, I called a staff meeting. WHAT? I never called staff meetings. I usually used a Monday Memo as our weekly portable staff meeting, but this was pivotal!

In the staff meeting, I explained that we had lacked a clear instructional model and that the campus leadership team worked to develop one for us.

Then, I carefully taught each of the tenets. I closed the meeting by giving the teachers their posters to hang in prominent places in their classrooms and explained that I would be teaching the instructional model to our students during Friday's Gober Facetime so that they understood why all of their teachers were being more diligent about "posting learning objectives," for example.

The following Monday, I published it again in the Monday Memo and in the campus newsletter for parents to see. I was serious about this—it was not a fad that would soon go away. But make no mistake; it was not the staff meeting, posters, or publishing in newsletters that were going to hold everyone accountable. I had one layer of accountability with the students, who would sometimes ask their teacher, "Where is the learning objective for today?" More than that, though, High Reliability Schools have evidence, a lagging indicator that shows that effective teaching, as defined in their instructional model, occurs in each classroom every day. This is where the instructional snapshot comes in.

Instructional Snapshots

I met with the leadership team again, and we took our instructional model and developed it into a walkthrough form. It was short, with a series of "look-fors" that administrators, instructional coaches, and department chairs answered by circling YES or NO.

On the triplicate form that we eventually turned into a Google Form, there was a place to write the name of the PLC or department, date, and class period. To reinforce our claim that this was non-evaluative, we did not write the name of the teacher. It took about five minutes to observe the items on our snapshot, and if a classroom was taking a summative-type assessment, we skipped that class and did not complete the snapshot.

I required ten snapshots, or "snaps," by the end of the day on Friday from each of my APs and Instructional Coaches. Collectively, that should bring in eighty snaps per week. I manually tallied up the snaps and included a summary in my Monday Memo that looked like Figure 9.2.

WHOA! I had my answer to the question, "What does instruction look like in our school?" It looked like over half the classrooms were not adhering to

Instructional Snapshot (Non-Evaluative)		
PLC/Dept: _____	Date: _____	Period: _____
Frame the Lesson	YES / NO	Learning objective posted or clearly inferred
	YES / NO	Learning activity is relevant
Optimize Learning Atmosphere	YES / NO	Classroom is safe and welcoming
	YES / NO	Use of available resources for optimal student learning
Collaborate and Engage	YES / NO	Learning activity provides opportunity for collaboration
	YES / NO	Learning activity was engaging for the students
Differentiate	YES / NO	Evidence of differentiation was observed
Write, Write and Reteach	YES / NO	Did the learning activity allow for student writing
	YES / NO	Evidence of early intervention and/or reteaching
IB-Related Items	YES / NO	Learning activity connected to the IB Learner Profile
	YES / NO	Evidence of current IB unit observed

Figure 9.1 Sample instructional snapshot.

the instructional model that we developed and agreed upon. I followed the reporting of the snap data with a few comments in the Monday Memo:

This was our first week implementing our Instructional Model and collecting data using Instructional Snapshots. As a reminder, an administrator or IC will randomly visit classrooms throughout the week to observe our collective campus instruction. Before leaving the room, they will leave a pink copy of the Snap form on your desk without disturbing you. Please be assured we are not using this data for evaluative purposes but to measure ourselves against our expectation for effective instruction in every classroom. This week, we observed 84 classrooms. Although I am proud to see that our classrooms are safe and welcoming, I can also see that we are not differentiating or writing. This week in your PLCs, be sure to discuss how your team will create learning experiences that meet the expectations of our campus Instructional Model.

The instructional snapshot walkthroughs add to your **Principal Presence**, and the weekly data adds to your **Principal Mystique**. I suggest you follow up the first week by attending as many PLCs as you can and taking more time than usual to leave comments for each PLC in the shared PLC templates

Instructional Snapshot (Non-Evaluative) Week 1 SUMMARY		
Frame the Lesson	31/84	Learning objective posted or clearly inferred
	20/84	Learning activity is relevant
Optimize Learning Atmosphere	81/84	Classroom is safe and welcoming
	39/84	Use of available resources for optimal student learning
Collaborate and Engage	19/84	Learning activity provides opportunity for collaboration
	21/84	Learning activity was engaging for the students
Differentiate	27/84	Evidence of differentiation was observed
Write, Write and Reteach	8/84	Did the learning activity allow for student writing
	11/84	Evidence of early intervention and/or reteaching
IB-Related Items	60/84	Learning activity connected to the IB Learner Profile
	58/84	Evidence of current IB unit observed

Figure 9.2 Instructional snapshot summary.

about your expectations to adhere to the instructional model. Always include snap data with a few comments in your Monday Memo. The instructional model is important and deserves **Principal Presence**.

Each year, during the summer, it is important to review your snapshot form and modify it as needed. Eventually, our snaps moved to Google Forms, which automatically sent a copy to the teacher and tallied the data for me. This saved us time tallying the results and allowed us to increase our snaps to 150 per week.

There is no correct or incorrect snapshot model. The key is that it should measure what is expected in the classroom. Later in my career, I was the principal supervisor for a campus that was 1:1 with student technology. That year, the campus added a "Technology Use" section to their snapshot. This is an appropriate addition because, with the investment in technology, teachers were expected to integrate student technology into their lessons.

In short, instructional snapshots hold a mirror in front of the staff that reflects what instruction looks like on campus. Assuming the snapshot is aligned to an agreed-upon instructional model, showing your teachers a summary of instructional snapshot data each week holds everyone accountable. There is no need for the snaps to be evaluative because most teachers know how they reflect in that "mirror," and supervisors can easily follow up with the teachers who fall behind with a crucial conversation and/or an evaluative observation.

Using PLCs, lesson plans, and my communication tools, I was able to impose my **Principal Presence** and expand my **Principal Mystique** to ultimately create a high-performing learning environment for my students. However, the instructional snapshot has proven to be the most useful tool in my instructional leadership toolbox.

10 **Data Monitoring**

Regular data monitoring needs a system, something that is practical and sustainable. It shouldn't make teachers think, "Big brother is watching," but rather "My principal is engaged."

DR. GOBER

Eating an Elephant

I admit that in my first few years as principal, I severely lacked in the area of data analysis. My excuse was not will or skill—it was solely the enormity of the task. There is so much data! I was haunted by district administrators who constantly reminded us principals about the importance of data-based decision-making. Of course, I wanted to make informed decisions that yielded more opportunities for success! Of course, I wanted to have the comfort and confidence that my decisions were informed by relevant data and that the tasks that followed my decisions would yield results! (One of my worst fears, by the way, was that a decision I made would inadvertently harm a student.) All the principals in the room seemed confident and unphased by this expectation to analyze the data and use it to make data-informed decisions. I had to hide my anxiety year after year because I felt I was weak in this area.

It was not until I had a conversation with a group of principals in the parking lot after a monthly principal meeting that I realized that everyone, including myself, used data to the best of their ability. Unless something was highlighted by the district, we all went back to our campuses and went through the motions of monitoring and reacting to data.

There's an old joke: "How do you eat an elephant? One bite at a time." As I developed as a principal, I constantly sought ways and tools to eat the proverbial elephant. I needed to figure out what constituted a "bite," and after five years or so, I defined "one bite at a time" with a two-part system: (1) learning which data needed to be monitored and how often, and (2) developing a system to quickly access the data, along with a team of data nerds to assist.

Once I completed the first step, I felt that I had cut up my bites and knew when to eat them. This task relieved my anxiety and added exponentially to my **Principal Mystique**, "he knows everything."

Dividing the elephant into bite-sized pieces and scheduling the bites is half of the system. You need a team for the other half. Creating a team provides multiple perspectives when digesting the data. By having a team, you will inevitably be forced to create a schedule for the team to meet, which holds you accountable.

Creating a data team should not be taken lightly. You want your brightest teachers as well as out-of-the-box thinkers. In short, you want data nerds! You can call it your Think Tank or your Data Dig Team, whatever you like. Ask for volunteers, but carefully select a small cadre of teachers (I recommend four to six) to help you analyze and dig through the data weekly. With some creative master scheduling, you may be able to align planning periods so the team can meet during the school day rather than after work.

Data Management

Today, there are many tools available to help you create your own "principal dashboard." The investment in an effective data management system is money well spent and will ultimately save hundreds of man-hours if a district is using data regularly. I recommend volunteering to serve on the district committee if and when your district is selecting a data management system to ensure the product is campus-friendly. You want a tool that provides live data with graphics and reports that are easy to create and read. I further recommend that the system allow teachers access to view all of the data available for their students.

Monitoring data should no longer be a herculean task, and whether it happens or not is a direct result of whether you, the principal, make it a priority. This is another case where people notice your presence, or lack of presence, and everyone aligns their actions to the expectations you set forth. Data deserves **Principal Presence**!

	Daily	Weekly	Grading Period	Semester	Annually
Attendance	X	X	X	X	X
Discipline Referrals	X	X	X	X	X
Course Failures	X	X	X	X	X
PLC Assessments (Formative and Summative)		X	X	X	X
Student Intervention Plans			X	X	X
Nationally Normed Tests (Academic Growth)			X	X	X
Students with Credit Deficiencies				X	X
State and National Assessments					X

Figure 10.1 Data monitoring frequency chart.

Inspect What You Expect

Monitoring data is not a passive task. Monitoring is analyzing and looking for trends, concerns, and celebrations and, when necessary, questioning the data for root cause analysis. There are many trainings you can attend on what to look for with each specific data set, but here is a broad perspective of what I looked for.

Attendance, Discipline, and Grades

Monitor this daily and encourage the teachers and APs to do the same. These three areas are crucial MTSS early warning indicators for students who may need some sort of intervention.

Create a dashboard that has warning thresholds for each area. For example, students who have a 10 percent or more absence rate, students with two or more discipline referrals, or students who are failing two or more courses. By creating an early warning system that you monitor daily, you can begin creating a list of students that you carry with you and ask questions about when you are with a counselor, AP, or the teachers of those students. You literally write down the top twenty students you are concerned about and make sure someone takes responsibility for getting an intervention plan developed and in place.

Sometimes, early detection can deter the need for an intervention. I met a principal who proactively attacked her attendance problem by promoting the benefits of having perfect attendance for the first thirty days of school. If any student was absent in the first thirty days of school, someone called their parent (within the first hour) to encourage them to come to school or find out exactly why they could not do so. The phone call was not punitive or demeaning; it was a care call. "It's 9:30, and we noticed that CJ is not at school. Is everything okay?" "As you know, we strive to have 100% attendance from every student for our first 30 days of school, so if she can make it to school, we will be that much closer to meeting our goal."

PLC Data (Formative and Summative)

Having access to all of the PLCs and the data teachers use to make instructional decisions is paramount to leading an effective school. Sometimes, teachers look at their data and either have blinders or filters on that prevent them from seeing their data objectively.

The biology teachers all know that the Genetics Unit is difficult for students, so when they look over the data from that unit, they are not surprised to see lower scores and passing rates. They write it off as, "It's the Genetics Unit, and our students always struggle." I do not have any judgment about this mindset—it is normal and natural, especially for experienced teachers. But I thought the data team might have a different perspective and be able to help.

After looking at the scope and sequence of the Genetics Unit, the data team proposed starting the unit with genetic mutations and hereditary traits. Traditionally, the unit began with vocabulary and understanding the molecular structure. For science teachers, it makes perfect sense to lay a foundation of knowledge before building up to the complexities of mutations. However, two of my data nerds were history and English teachers who strongly believed that if the students were more intrigued with the subject and could relate to having "mom's red hair" or "dad's connected earlobes," they would be more engaged for this unit of study. Another suggestion was to create exit tickets as common formative assessments (CFA) so the teachers would know exactly what concepts were troublesome for the students. Using CFAs allows teachers to remediate quickly during the next day's instruction. We had to wait a year for the biology teachers to try these suggestions, but when they did, they saw better outcomes and evidence of more learning.

The other issue for PLCs regarding analyzing their data is time. They simply do not have enough time dedicated to reviewing all available data. The data team understands that and can observe that 90 percent of the students passed a unit test and that the team moved on to the next unit. The data team looked not only at the 10 percent who did not pass but also identified three questions on the test that more than 40 percent of the students answered incorrectly. Those three questions were measuring the same learning objective and therefore . . . "We have a problem!" Almost half of our students did not understand this learning objective!

Monitoring PLC data adds to your **Principal Presence** and **Principal Mystique**. "Wow, I did not know he looked at our data that closely." This reaction results in, "We need to look closer at our data." And that result came from teachers, not you, so your high expectations gain momentum and create synergy.

Interventions

I must admit that managing interventions has been a work in progress for much of my principal career. Here again, the advancements in technology and educational tools developed specifically for MTSS and intervention management make this monitoring task more palatable and efficient than it used to be. Now, with the proper tools, you can not only review who has an intervention plan, but you can also look at the plan to inspect the goals and see which staff member is responsible for monitoring.

As principal, your role with intervention plans is to ensure that students who need interventions are getting them and that the staff has the time and resources necessary to implement the plans. Your review of this each grading period keeps your staff on their toes and serves as another level of monitoring for students who need interventions. When implementing MTSS, it is helpful to set goals for your staff. For example, "We will have intervention plans developed by the end of the second grading period for at least 80% of our students who need Tier 2 academic interventions." Setting this type of goal keeps you and your staff focused on identifying students early.

State and National Norm-Referenced Assessments

These tests are often given two or more times per school year. They assess for language acquisition, reading proficiency levels, academic progress or growth, and many other annual assessments that are usually district mandated. As a data team, we looked at these data from a campus level as it became available. Of course, teachers and other staff members were taught how to read the scores and how to use the information to inform their decision-making. But as the principal, you need to become familiar with and eventually master the data from these assessments. Your ability to interpret the data to assist staff with student interventions and instructional strategies will not go unnoticed. You are the principal, the *principal-teacher*, the *principal-learner*, and the *principal-statistician*.

Asking Questions of Your Data

As you sit in PLCs, review lesson plans, analyze your data, and listen to your staff, you will naturally come up with numerous questions. This was my favorite part of studying my campus data. I loved to challenge myself and my Data Dig Team with queries that our data should be able to answer. A few examples were:

1. What is the correlation between our In-School Suspension roster and our state assessment failure roster?
2. In the last three years, which week or month had the lowest attendance rate? What units are being taught in our core subjects during that time? How well did our students do on those assessments?
3. Which teacher has the most students that showed growth between the Beginning of Year and Middle of Year, according to our academic growth assessments?

4. Who has the highest average PSAT score among the students who play defense versus offense on our football team?

One of my assistant principals loved this and aptly noted that there should be a position, perhaps even a district department, created to ask questions about the data. The number of questions is infinite and perhaps worthy of a separate book. But be careful not to ask questions that may reveal only problems (examples 1 and 2). Have fun with your data and find some fun or noteworthy news as well (examples 3 and 4). Whatever you find, share it in your Monday Memo with the staff (if appropriate) and ask your staff to ask questions for the Data Dig Team to answer. Create a culture that is truly data conscious and savvy.

Red Bears

When I became a principal supervisor, my experience was solely at the secondary level. I decided to work closely with my elementary schools to see how the Gober Five would work at their campuses. Of course, I taught all my principals about creating systems for communication, lesson planning, PLCs, analyzing data, and snapshots, but I truly enjoyed watching the elementary campuses implement these systems. I had heard of campuses using data walls, but I thought that technology tools had made this practice obsolete. Not so. Literally, they used their whole wall. One principal shared with me that she wanted to "see" all of her students and where they stood academically. That data wall was in her office, so student success, or lack thereof, was in her face all day, every day. She installed curtains to cover the wall when she had people in her office who were not privy to the data.

Her mascot was a bear, so each of her 400 students' names was on a green, yellow, or red bear that correlated to students who met mastery, were close to meeting mastery, or had yet to meet mastery, respectively. The color was determined by how they did on the previous year's state assessment in math and reading. She then used district assessments that aligned to the state assessment to measure her students throughout the year. All of the teachers' formative and summative assessments had to align to the state assessment, and at the end of each week, the teachers came into her office to update the students (bears) on her wall.

Week to week, only a few changes were made, but over the course of the year, she wanted to see those red bears turn into yellow bears and eventually green bears. Her wall was divided by grade level and teacher. On Fridays, usually after school, the teachers scurried in there to update their bears, making sure their principal noticed when a bear changed its color. Of course, the occasional green bear turning yellow got the principal's immediate attention, and she usually addressed it by looking at that teacher's lesson plan and PLC notes to ensure that the student's needs were being addressed. She would expect to see an intervention plan for that student, a record of parent contact, and evidence that this student was not getting left behind.

This elementary principal owned monitoring data and required her teachers to own it as well. When the teachers know the principal is focused on student achievement and growth, they will become focused on it, too, and their planning and lessons will reflect that.

Knowing Students by Name and Need

I don't know who said it first, but the words are abundantly clear and too important not to repeat. **You need to know every student by name and need**! I first heard this spoken by a principal to her teachers. The staff knew this principal was a "data queen" who studied the state assessments and knew her state's accountability system. She was highly proficient in the state learning objectives, how often those learning objectives were tested, and how they were tested.

This principal would not dare entertain the idea of a data wall. She was all about binders! Each grade level had a binder. At the front of each binder were the learning objectives and released copies of the state assessments. Behind those were tabs with each teacher's name, and each student had a page in their teacher's section. The student data page had the essential student demographic information and a data history that was printed out from the district's data management system. The principal went through each student's page with their teacher prior to the first day of school, making notes on the pages to summarize each student's needs. She didn't leave it to chance—her teachers would study each student's data to not only know them by name but also know them by need on the first day of school.

Predicting Your Accountability

Every school has some level of accountability. Whatever that accountability system looks like, it is imperative that at least one person on that campus truly understands that system. They should be monitoring the data throughout the school year and be able to make a sound prediction at any point about their accountability rating, score, or outcome. And that one person should always be the principal!

I am amazed at how many principals cannot answer the question, "If you were assessed today, what would your rating be?" Monitoring, analyzing, and interpreting your data throughout the school year will allow you to answer that question and hundreds more.

The Data Dig Team and I challenged ourselves to predict the school's accountability each grading period using the data we had available at that time of year. Over time, we became very accurate.

It is not enough for the principal to be able to predict the campus's accountability. Each teacher should be expected to predict their students' success and be able to show why. When test results are released, analyze teacher predictions versus actual grades and work with your staff to better calibrate. An effective model of teacher grade prediction is found with the International Baccalaureate (IB) Diploma Programme.

> *The International Baccalaureate (IB) Diploma Programme requires teachers to predict their students' final exam scores midway through the course. These predictions are based on the teacher's understanding of IB standards, student performance, potential growth, and other factors. IB provides tailored data on predicted grades for each subject, helping even new teachers make accurate forecasts. Teachers work with IB coordinators to improve their prediction accuracy, which is a key indicator of an effective IB teacher. This system helps students better understand their academic progress during the rigorous program. ("Discover Why IB Students Succeed," 2024)*

Can you imagine a school where students monitor their progress and are taught about the different assessments they take to make predictions about their final grade, state assessment score, or college entry exam outcome? What if the teachers at that same school made those same types of predictions for each of their students? And can you imagine what would happen if their principal processed the data and understood the accountability system for her campus to serve as a live barometer for that school's accountability? That would be an effective school! That would be an effective principal!

Part III
The Predictable Principal

11 **Your Consistency**

Leadership falls into two categories. Those who are inconsistent, whose actions cannot be predicted, who agree today on a major [issue] and repudiate it the following day. Those who are consistent, who have a sense of honour, a vision.
NELSON MANDELA

Being Predictable

I have always defined my style of leadership as being closely aligned to the servant-leadership model. I take pride in knowing I went up through the ranks of school administration, and I can often relate to the challenges faced by most educators. I recall that as I developed as a leader, I read books and did coursework focused on the importance of having a clear mission and vision. I read about being transformational and innovative and had the great fortune of serving under leaders who were truly phenomenal. I have also had the misfortune of working for leaders who were narcissists, micromanagers, and, worst of all, unpredictable.

While in graduate school, I came across an article published in the July–August 1995 issue of *Harvard Business Review* titled "The Power of Predictability." Admittedly, I had never thought about the importance of being predictable. My first thought of being a predictable leader conjured images of a simple, inept, underqualified person. After all, shouldn't a leader keep everyone on their toes and create an atmosphere that is free from being bland and boring? Have we not all heard that being comfortable can bring about complacency and, ultimately, underperformance?

The authors describe the early days of humanity and outline how early hunters and gatherers needed predictability as a matter of human survival. The conclusion of the article offered a warning about life without predictability.

> *Human beings have finite energy and finite time in which to expend it. The more that managers make clear to employees and other stakeholders which courses of action will improve their lives, the more that employees can focus*

on creating value. What our ancestors discovered holds true today: Survival still depends on the ability to respond quickly to change, and organizations can still help people predict the outcomes of their actions and thus act swiftly and predictably. Without predictability, people will be too scared not only to take risks but to take any actions at all. Life within an organization will become what it was for the solitary hunter: uncertain, brutish, and short. (p. 148–9)

When I think back on some of the great teachers I have had, great leaders I have worked for, and even colleagues and friends who I thought were phenomenal leaders, one of the common characteristics is that they were all very predictable. You know what predictable leaders want and expect from you and others. You know what they consider when they make decisions. You know what upsets them or makes them proud. You always know where you stand; therefore, you can take on more challenges and risks because it is safe to do so. These leaders have systems, and their professional lives are organized and balanced and bring a sense of safety and comfort to all those around them. They are predictable not only in their words and actions but also in their reactions. Working with them is empowering, liberating, and safe.

Being predictable means being consistent, and consistency doesn't mean being rigid and unchanging, having an uninspiring routine, or not being invested in your work or career. Being predictable is about having systems that allow you to organize your work environment so that you and all stakeholders flourish in a comfortable and safe setting. This is part of your **Principal Presence**—the systems you establish and maintain are high priorities for you. Let them speak for you each and every day.

When your coaches and sponsors send you briefs and updates to add to your newsletter, they are using your system. Your expectation that they send you updates comes with a tool, process, and schedule that makes it very easy for them to comply. When your teachers are meeting in PLCs or completing their lesson plan, your **Principal Presence** lingers in their subconscious to comply at first and eventually to impress and seek your approval. When your APs, ICs, and department chairs review data and discover a hidden problem or celebration, your **Principal Presence** manifests itself because they know it was your insistence and expectation that they spend the time reviewing data. And, of course, whether you or someone else completes an instructional snapshot, everyone knows that not only are snapshots conducted because you expect it, but also that you review snapshot data regularly, highlighting areas of growth and exceptionalism.

Creating systems that make sense and ultimately enhance the work lives of your staff and the success of your students is difficult work to start. Being consistent in the implementation of those systems is even more difficult, but it brings about predictability. The blogger Todd Ordal writes, "Predictability means being the same leader in crisis as you are in calm, providing a steady hand that guides rather than jerks the wheel" (Ordal, 2024).

Furthermore, your collective **Principal Presence** is a significant contributor to your **Principal Mystique**. Consider the impact of your leadership style on your school's culture. A culture that's built with stability and predictability fosters an environment where teachers feel safe to innovate, take risks, and challenge the status quo. This culture is healthy and positive, and it provides a competitive advantage that will ultimately add to your **Principal Mystique**.

Being Unpredictable

I know a school leader who, during a staff meeting, asked for feedback on how she was doing as a leader. After they had finished providing feedback, some of which was obviously a surprise to the leader, she thanked them and stated that she would be sure to reflect on what she learned. She ended the meeting by stating that while she was reflecting, everyone else should reflect on whether they were a good fit for her team or not. Wait, what? A huge part of the feedback was about her constant unpredictability, unclear expectations, and lack of consistency. She was so blind to her unpredictability that she did not realize that her response not only manifested her narcissism, but it also showed that the only thing about her leadership that was predictable was her unpredictability.

Dealing with an unpredictable leader is exhausting and challenging. They create havoc and remove the feeling of safety—a key need for a team and culture to survive and thrive. When principals are unpredictable, it leads to a school culture of anxiety and mistrust. Staff and teachers may become hesitant to take initiative or make decisions, fearing the unknown reaction of their principal. Amy Edmonson's TEDx talk from 2014 called "Building a Psychologically Safe Workplace" is a valuable resource to tap into to learn more about the importance of psychological safety in an organization.

Most leaders who are not predictable are completely unaware of the impact of their unpredictability. I want to encourage you to be open to feedback and honest dialogue with the people you serve. Be open to stakeholder perspectives and criticism. This not only helps you grow as a leader but also strengthens the trust and bond they all will have with you.

In Chapter 6, "Communication," I outlined three models that I used to communicate with stakeholders. But take note that each model also allowed for open and anonymous stakeholder feedback. Effective principals must be open to feedback, and those who are not will always struggle in their leadership. An effective way to assess your predictability is to constantly seek feedback. Once you get feedback, truly think about what is being stated and why. Think about what people are not telling you. And never forget—most people, especially educators, are not trying to hurt you. When (not if) you receive criticism, know that someone was bold and brave enough to bring that critical feedback to your attention. Now you have the opportunity to further enhance your **Principal Mystique** by self-reflecting and self-correcting. Here are some real examples of the power of soliciting feedback:

- "Thank you for changing the PLC template to add drop-down menus. It significantly reduces our time to do this."
- "I knew you were the best principal. Thanks for allowing us to eat outside and please know that I am writing the PTA to thank them for the new tables. My classroom does not have windows, so this means a lot to me!"
- "Thank you for adding more visitor spots in the parking lot. It was such a nuisance to come to the campus when there was nowhere to park."
- "I know it was hard to admit your mistake, but it says a lot about who you are and I am proud to call you my boss. We will all help fix the schedule."
- "Thank you! I am tired of not seeing anyone else in my hall stand outside their doors between classes. I am not sure what you did or said, but it worked (and I know you know it because I noticed you a few days coming down here to check things out). You're the best, yes it was me that sent that message."

I could fill twenty pages with these real responses to changes that I have made due to mostly anonymous feedback. Responding to the feedback was something everyone knew I would do. It was predictable. Therefore, I received more feedback and made more changes to create a better school and workplace.

Catchphrases Lead to Predictability

Harry Wong stated that "A well-managed classroom is a task-oriented and predictable environment" (2005, p. 88). Children thrive in predictable environments. Consider parents of toddlers who discover the terrible twos; parents who have created clear boundaries and established routines with consistent schedules usually breeze through these years and find them to be very enjoyable and full of fun. However, those parents who have yet to create predictability and consistency for their little ones find these years to be difficult, stressful, and never-ending. We all know both types of parents, and if you can't think of any, a quick visit to your local grocery store on a Saturday afternoon will give you plenty of fodder for your own research.

Adults are no different. Just like Dr. Wong taught us to create predictable classrooms, the principal must create a predictable school not only for the students but also for the staff. As principal, I found that over time, I received fewer and fewer complaints and inquiries from both staff and parents. Someone jokingly said to me, "I know what you are going to say, but I just thought I would ask anyway." I discovered that I repeated the same phrases, and eventually, even staff members and students would say them to each other.

I compiled a list of phrases that became my signature or catchphrases during my principalship:

1. Don't solve problems with email.
2. Don't blame the students.
3. Did you read the Monday Memo?
4. Think and link. (If you are thinking about changing a routine or system, link up with those whom it will impact.)
5. No surprises! (No one likes to be surprised by information you could have prepared them for.)
6. Fix the systems, not the people.
7. Win the students, and the parents will fall in line. (Become a student magnet.)
8. Your presence is noticed. Your absence is noticed.
9. What you spend your time and money on is what you value.

10. The classroom is sacred. PLC time is sacred.

11. Use bullets, not paragraphs. (Be succinct in what you are saying.)

12. I would rather rein you in than have to keep on pushing you.

13. I'm joking, but I'm not joking. (I might say it in a fun manner, but I am not joking.)

14. What's in you will come out of you. (Any biases or bigotry you have will eventually come out. Work on yourself.)

15. Don't email all if only two people need to be told something.

16. Don't call a meeting when an email will suffice.

17. Is it good for our students?

18. What does the data say?

19. I don't know, but I will find out.

20. Make sure you follow up.

Most issues are not new issues. Since I strived to be predictable and consistent, I normally responded to the crisis of the day the same way I did the last time that crisis came up. This is not to say that I was never stumped or surprised. When a new crisis reared its head, I may not have had a packaged response ready (if "I don't know, but I will find out" does not work), so I did my best to buy time until I could bring this crisis to my admin team for us to find a solution. The response of seeking help, seeking advice, admitting that I didn't know, and showing that I would help find a solution was predictable.

And after a solution or response is found—make sure you follow up!

It is humbling for me as a parent to realize that, in some ways, I have become my parents. "I am going to put a fire in you or under you" came out of my mouth when an attempt to motivate my son one day turned into frustration. I stopped dead in my tracks in awe of how naturally that happened, and I had to concede that "I've become my dad." If my dad only knew, he would be beaming with pride. As a principal, you will feel this same pride when teachers and campus leaders say and do things because they always hear and see them from you. Wow. Now, your systems are *how we do school*, and even your personality and likeness are becoming inextricably woven into the fabric of the school culture (**Principal Presence**). Predictability is powerful.

12 **Your Time**

I don't have time to find time for what is important, it's already on my calendar.
DR. GOBER

Schedule Your Priorities

A new principal came to shadow me once. At the end of the day, he stated that I make everything look so easy and I have a reputation for never being stressed. Well, both are false, but I can understand why that perception existed—it was my **Principal Mystique**. I would never say things were easy, but I would say that I always tried to find ways to make things easier. There is no better way to illustrate that than to look at a typical month's schedule. I carefully analyzed my time and created a schedule and routine that I rarely strayed from. I put into practice Stephen Covey's third habit, "Put First Things First." As Covey explains, "The key is not to prioritize what's on your schedule, but to schedule your priorities" (Covey 1989, p. 161). By understanding all of my systems and expectations, I put into practice what I constantly preached: you spend your time (and money) on what you value.

My calendar was always up-to-date, and I lived religiously by my calendar. I shared it with the staff so that everyone knew where to find me and could clearly see what was important to me by how I scheduled my time. Over the years, not only did my staff know key elements of my calendar, but even parents, students, and the district office knew. For example, my principal supervisor, superintendent, and the school board knew that on Friday mornings, I talked with my students via Gober Facetime. Parents knew that I would send the newsletter on Monday by noon. Teachers knew that I reviewed lesson plans and monitored PLCs on Friday afternoons. My time was predictable.

Let's look at the days of the week and what was scheduled for each day. Your week may not look like my week, but I'm including a sample week and my reasons for scheduling this way. As a leader, you will need to think through your priorities and how to meet with everyone who needs a bit of your time.

I color coded my calendar: a red meeting was a meeting that I absolutely could not miss. If I had to miss this meeting, it would need to be canceled. Light red events were usually campus events. An AP could cover blue meetings for me when necessary, or the meetings could be canceled or rescheduled. Yellow meetings were optional, and I usually didn't know if I would attend these until the last minute, so I started to pencil them on my calendar.

Sample Week

Monday (Meetings Day)

I dreaded Mondays, but I loved Mondays. I dreaded Mondays for the same reason most people do—the weekend family time was over, and I absolutely had to get up and get moving because there was a lot to do. Also, Mondays and Fridays were too important for me to miss. I couldn't be sick. I couldn't be late. This was the day for meetings, and a full day of meetings is hard.

But I loved Mondays because those meetings were *my* meetings, and best of all, by the end of the day, I had met with all of my leaders and student groups. (You may need to revisit Chapter 5, "First Things First—Organize Your Organization," for a reminder about how I organized my staff into teams.) Lastly, I loved Mondays because there were usually no after-school events. I knew I could go home at a decent hour.

> **8:00–10:00 a.m. and 1:00–2:00 p.m.: Meetings**, which included administration team, leadership teams, following up on student concerns, reviewing the Monday Memo and Campus Newsletter, monthly meetings with counselors and student groups: Student Advisory (1st Monday of the Month), Student Club Presidents (2nd Monday), School Counselors (3rd Monday), and Student Council (4th Monday).

> **11:00 a.m.: Lunch Supervision.** Every day except Wednesday, I ate my lunch in the cafeteria as I supervised the lunch periods. This two-hour block of time consisted of me at a lunch table with a laptop and lunch, working on various issues. I walked around, talking and checking in on students **(Principal Presence).** I also told staff that if they wanted to meet with me, this was a great time to do so as long as they didn't mind eating with me in the cafeteria.

2:00–4:00 p.m.: Visit PLCs and conduct Instructional Snapshots for the rest of the day.

Tuesday (Open Day)

For the most part, Tuesdays were open during the day, and I had meetings after school and in the evenings.

8:00 a.m.–4:00 p.m.: Open all day (but always supervise lunch if possible). I planned it like this because I realized that after all of my Monday meetings, I needed time for the work that manifested itself in Monday's meetings. This included any feedback from students, parents, or staff who may have used the anonymous online feedback form.

4:00 p.m.: New Teacher Training (2nd Tuesday) **or Leadership Training** (4th Tuesday). I held two to three days of summer training and activities that familiarized the New Teachers with the campus and monthly meetings to enhance and maintain that training throughout the year. I tried to align the monthly meetings to what was going on at that point in the year. For example, the September meeting discussed the philosophy of grading, athletic eligibility, and preparing for teacher conferences. The February meeting went over understanding the teacher evaluation system and how to improve in growth areas.

For the fourth Tuesday Leadership Trainings, I covered a variety of topics. The most popular were communication strategies, getting organized, understanding assessments, and growing effective teachers. This meeting was for all of my APs as well as any staff member who expressed interest in becoming an administrator. The first year, I only had two teachers attend, but over time, it grew to about a dozen teachers. This is an investment that pays off exponentially over time and adds to your **Principal Presence**. Developing and growing your staff, especially your aspiring leaders, will keep your superstar staff members professionally "fed." You will be able to ensure the sustainability of the systems you put in place by teaching them more about what they are and how to use them.

10:00 a.m. and/or 5:00 p.m.: PTA/Booster Club President Meetings were held only once a month, and I scheduled them on the same day as PTA/Booster Club meetings.

6:00 p.m.: PTA or Booster Club Meetings (1st and 3rd Tuesday) or **School Board Meetings** (2nd and 4th Tuesdays) School Board meetings were not mandatory for me to attend, but there were times that I was asked to attend or present, and other times I wanted to attend because I was just curious about something. I added them to my calendar more as placeholders in case I needed to be there.

Wednesday (District Day)

I dedicated every Wednesday to the district because I was required to attend biweekly district meetings that were already scheduled. But every principal knows or will quickly learn that the district office loves to call meetings. I let it be known that I was not available on Mondays or Fridays and had set aside every Wednesday just for them. Those district leaders who were organized and always well planned appreciated this. But district leaders who were constantly in crisis detested my insistence that I not be pulled off campus except for Wednesdays unless it was a true emergency. Of course, I encouraged anyone from the district office to come and visit me any day between 11 and 1 to meet and assist during lunch duty. I never got too many takers for that, or perhaps there were never any emergencies between 11 and 1 at the district office.

8:00 a.m.: District meetings every other week (following School Board Meetings)

12:00 p.m.: I had a boss who was a bonafide foodie and would love to "pick my brain" or ask "a small favor" while trying one of the many restaurants in our metro area. I eventually gave in and penciled in one hour following the District Meetings for him in case he wanted it.

Afternoons: Open unless someone at the district office scheduled a meeting. I tried to use this time to either catch up or complete formal teacher evaluations. Sometimes, I would visit classrooms for "Caught Ya Teaching" photos or video footage (Chapter 6), catch up on my instructional snapshots, or look over PLC meeting notes and provide feedback, thus enhancing my **Principal Mystique**. If I actually conducted a formal observation or went into classrooms for snapshots or walkthroughs, I simply changed the blue on my calendar to red. No one was ever allowed to take me out of a classroom unless there was a true emergency.

6:00 p.m.: Possible campus event (concert, college fair, et cetera)

Thursday (Open Day)

Much like Tuesday, Thursday mornings were wide open, and I purposely tried to be out in the halls and classrooms as much as possible. In the afternoon, I met with my data team (Chapter 10, "Data Monitoring"), and the two hours we set aside for this were never enough. My head was usually spinning after this meeting, but I set aside a special one-hour block after school to have one-on-one conversations with department chairs, instructional coaches, and other campus leaders. My goal was to meet with each one once per semester.

11:00 a.m.: Cafeteria supervision

2:00 p.m.: Data Dig Team to review various campus data (Chapter 10)

4:00 p.m.: One-on-one meetings with campus leaders

6:00 p.m.: Possible campus event (concert, college fair, etc.)

Friday (Catch Up and Prepare for Next Week)

Yay! It's Friday, and I loved Fridays because I had been pondering the whole week what I would discuss with the students during Gober Facetime (**Principal Presence**). Although I didn't schedule it on my calendar, the truth is from about 9:00 to 9:45, I was putting my final touches on my weekly message. I tried to make it humorous but ensured I conveyed high expectations for academics, attendance, and behavior. I always acknowledged athletic and fine arts competitions and ended with my tagline, "Make good decisions." Immediately after my time in the studio, I began the frantic rush to review lesson plans to provide feedback (**Principal Presence**), and if I was not able to make my assigned PLC this week, I reviewed those minutes and provided feedback while randomly picking another PLC to review so I could leave a few notes and enhance my **Principal Presence** and **Principal Mystique**.

I subscribed to the open-door policy, just as many leaders do, except for Friday afternoons. Frankly, I needed to focus on preparing for all of Monday's meetings, update the Monday Memo and School Newsletter, and respond to any pending emails or matters that I did not get to that week. This time was scheduled from 1:00–4:00 p.m., but most days I didn't finish until 7:00 p.m., and that worked out fine because then I could go straight to the varsity athletic event.

9:45: Gober Facetime, my weekly student communication.

11:00 a.m.: Cafeteria supervision. On Fridays, I tried to devote the time to "chopping it up" with my APs. We discussed the latest gossip, rumors, crises, and, of course, the latest strategies and best practices in school improvement.

1:00 p.m.: Catch up on lesson plan feedback and prepare for Monday.

6:00 p.m.: Possible campus event (concert, college fair, etc.).

7:00 p.m.: Varsity athletics. It was rare for me to miss a Friday night game.

This was my schedule each week. I made time for everything that was important while ensuring I had enough flexibility and open time for inevitable emergencies that arose. I fully admit that during my first few years as a principal, I did not have any sense of a system for anything. I was going through the motions in the "fake it until you make it" mindset. Those years were exhausting, and I was constantly on high alert and laser-focused on the matter at hand. In my mind, I was an ineffective principal.

It took approximately ten years as a principal to fully understand the importance of taking control of my time and not constantly being in crisis. Once I took control of my time, I was able to focus that time on systems that made sense and priorities that were important for student success.

MONDAY	TUESDAY	WEDNESDAY	THURSDAY	FRIDAY
8-10 Admin Team 10-11 Leadership Team 11-1 Newsletters/Lunch 1-2 Student Advisory 2-3 PLC Visits 3-4 Instructional Snapshots	8-10 OPEN 11-1 Lunch/Cafeteria Duty 1-4 OPEN 5-6 PTA President 6-7 PTA Meeting	8-12 District Principals Mtg 12-1 Lunch with Boss 1-4 OPEN	8-11 OPEN 11-1 Lunch/Cafeteria Duty 1-2 OPEN 2-4 Data Dig Team 4-5 Leaders 1:1	8-9 OPEN 9:45 Gober Facetime 10-11 Lesson Plans 11-1 Lunch/Cafeteria Duty 1-4 Catch Up 7-10 Varsity Athletics
7-8 Parent Coffee 8-10 Admin 10-11 Leadership 11-1 Newsletters/Lunch 1-2 Student Club Presidents 2-3 PLC Visits 3-4 Instructional Snapshots	8-10 OPEN 11-1 Lunch/Cafeteria Duty 1-4 OPEN 4-5 New Teacher Training 5:30 School Board Meeting	8-11 OPEN 11-1 Lunch/Cafeteria Duty 1-4 OPEN	8-11 OPEN 11-1 Lunch/Cafeteria Duty 1-2 OPEN 2-4 Data Dig Team 4-5 Leaders 1:1	8-9 OPEN 9:45 Gober Facetime 10-11 Lesson Plans 11-1 Lunch/Cafeteria Duty 1-4 Catch Up 7-10 Varsity Athletics
8-10 Admin 10-11 Leadership 11-1 Newsletters/Lunch 1-2 Counselors 2-3 PLC Visits 3-4 Instructional Snapshots	8-10 OPEN 11-1 Lunch/Cafeteria Duty 1-4 OPEN 5-6 Booster Club President 6-7 Booster Club Meeting	8-12 District Principals Mtg 12-1 Lunch w/ Boss 1-4 OPEN	8-11 OPEN 11-1 Lunch/Cafeteria Duty 1-2 OPEN 2-4 Data Dig Team 4-5 Leaders 1:1	8-9 OPEN 9:45 Gober Facetime 10-11 Lesson Plans 11-1 Lunch/Cafeteria Duty 1-4 Catch Up 7-10 Varsity Athletics
8-10 Admin 10-11 Leadership 11-1 Newsletters/Lunch 1-2 Student Council 2-3 PLC Visits 3-4 Instructional Snapshots	8-10 OPEN 11-1 Lunch/Cafeteria Duty 1-4 OPEN 4-5 Lessons in Leadership 5:30 School Board Meeting	8-11 OPEN 11-1 Lunch/Cafeteria Duty 1-4 OPEN	8-11 OPEN 11-1 Lunch/Cafeteria Duty 1-2 OPEN 2-4 Data Dig Team 4-5 Leaders 1:1	8-9 OPEN 9:45 Gober Facetime 10-11 Lesson Plans 11-1 Lunch/Cafeteria Duty 1-4 Catch Up 7-10 Varsity Athletics

Figure 12.1 Sample principal's monthly calendar.

Here is a look at a monthly calendar. Some things would be added, like school events and meetings with parents, but those things would not cause me to cancel or move my "red" scheduled items. My front office staff and APs were all aware of how I managed my time, and they perfected the art of scheduling around my priorities. One thing to note is that all after-school events would always start at 6:00 p.m. Families and community members appreciated the consistency (and predictability) of this standard. Athletics were the exception to this rule.

Not Everything Is an Emergency

It is hard for a fuming parent to understand that the principal cannot drop everything and hear their complaint as soon as they walk in the door. It is difficult for a teacher who wants some coaching or needs to vent to comprehend why the principal can't drop everything to listen. It is frustrating for someone from the district office to call or drop by the campus to share some feedback or express a concern to find out that you are not available. These scenarios and many others are valid, perhaps even urgent, reasons to meet with the principal. But they are NOT emergencies.

I always talked to my front office staff about my calendar and what constituted an emergency sufficient to take me out of one of my meetings. I explained my color-coded system and that, ideally, I did not want anything canceled or rescheduled. If someone absolutely could not meet with me on the times available Tuesday through Friday and Monday was the only day, then cancel or reschedule anything after 12:00 p.m. My Monday morning items could not be canceled or rescheduled unless the building was on fire, we had a safety or security concern, or one of my bosses gave me a clear directive to stop what I was doing.

This is an important conversation to have and perhaps have often, not only with your front office staff but also with yourself. "Emergencies" cannot keep distracting you from communicating with your students or reviewing lesson plans, monitoring data, and developing yourself and others as instructional leaders. "Emergencies" cannot keep you out of the classrooms and in the dark about what instruction looks like on your campus.

There may be some resentment, and certainly there are legitimate exceptions, but staying true to your schedule and your priorities will ultimately reduce the number of emergencies, complaints, and inquiries that come your way. People will see you more as a calm, collected, confident leader who has systems in place and a plan at hand. They will see that you put your students and teachers first and that they may need to plan better if they need your assistance. A calendar that prioritizes what is important for your students and staff adds a layer of lacquer to your image of being an effective principal. Slow down and stop the madness; schedule your priorities, then prioritize your schedule.

13 Your Legacy

Let my systems, not my name, be my legacy.
When you start your principal career, you don't think too much about your legacy. As you become more experienced and comfortable with your leadership abilities and begin thinking of your next career step (retirement or going to district administration), you wonder if you will leave a legacy and, if so, what it will be. This thought is quickly sobered by the reality that everyone, including you, is replaceable. But take a minute and truly ponder— what do you want your legacy to be? Will the relationships you developed, the aspiring leaders you tried to grow, the systems you implemented, and the expectations you've instilled have a positive and lasting effect? After leaving three different campuses as principal, I have learned that there are two types of legacies for the school principal. One is your personal legacy or what people think of you. The second is your institutional legacy, which consists of the systems, traditions, or practices you implemented that continue after you leave.

Personal Legacy

For your personal legacy, know that despite being the great principal you know you are, it will fade fast. Your personal legacy is determined by the relationships you have fostered with the staff—all of the staff. I recall being at a campus with a custodian who had been there for thirty years. Occasionally, I would share an early morning cup of coffee with her and listen to the stories she recounted about the principals she had seen come and go:

> And everyone loved Mr. Ross. He would always walk the halls, and in those days, we only had two lunches. Before 4th period, he would always be yelling out, "Feed your mind or feed your belly, let's go!" He was always saying fun things to keep the kids in line and motivated.

> Whew, Mr. Smith! That man ran the school like a drill sergeant. He did not play, no sir! You see all these clocks in every hallway? He did that. He expected these halls empty when that bell rang. The kids did not like him, and the staff was

scared of him. I did not care for him either because he was always fussing at me to fix these stupid clocks; some ran fast, and some ran slow. Yeah, I am glad he's gone.

Now, Mrs. Little was plain crazy, but I loved that crazy lady. She turned the old teacher's lounge into a computer lab. She is also the one that started requiring the teachers to meet with her at the end of each grading period to explain the low or failing grades for each of their students. Yeah, that Mrs. Little was tough on the teachers, but after we received that recognition from the state, she went to the district office. She is a sharp lady.

Never forget that you are in a people business. How you treat people will have the most influence on your personal legacy. Your presence or lack thereof will be noticed and remembered.

I will never forget the teacher who honestly could not say much about a previous principal because she never saw him. She could only recall the countless emails he would send the staff all day: "He never left his office, and he loved to bark out demands in emails that he would send to the whole staff. If there was ever a problem, even if it only had to do with one teacher, he would email the whole staff. Everyone hated that, and he never knew anyone's name."

If the staff thinks highly of you and knows you were fair, personable, supportive, and VISIBLE, they will hold your name in high regard, and perhaps a story about you will grow into a legend. I once met a young teacher who was at a school where I was formerly a principal. He rushed up to me and said, "I have heard so many stories about you. Did you really hide on the roof to catch kids leaving early?" What? Is that what is said about me? I laughed and simply said, "Yeah, that's me." But the truth is that I was on the roof with one of the maintenance workers because I wanted him to show me why the rooftop air conditioner kept breaking down. While I was up there, I saw a group of boys running from a side door. I yelled out to them by name and told them to meet me at their AP's office. "Dang, Gober be everywhere."

Principal Mystique!

I started this book by referencing how Peter DeWitt, a former K-5 public school principal-turned-author, presenter, and leadership coach, aptly noted in an *EdWeek* opinion piece that Todd Whitaker "already said it" (DeWitt, 2012). DeWitt was implying that everything to know about teacher and principal leadership has been covered by Todd Whitaker, who, in that same year, published two bestsellers—*What Great Teachers Do Differently* and *What Great Principals Do Differently*. In *What Great Teachers Do Differently*, Whitaker devoted the second chapter to explaining why "It's never about programs; it's always about people" (p. 8). An effective principal understands that and does not subscribe to the belief that "Gober's Five Systems" or "Whitaker's 17 Things That Matter Most" will improve schools or grow teachers without investing in people. The investment in developing healthy professional relationships with your staff and getting in the trenches with them so you understand how to help and support them is what really moves the school effectiveness needle. Your personal legacy should show that you grew and invested in your people and developed effective systems where students and staff alike would become successful.

Institutional Legacy

The other type of legacy is subtler and often nameless. I use institutional legacy to refer to changes that were made and continue, but no one remembers how they started. For example, the Monday Memo for staff is not a tool I invented. This portable faculty meeting was used in my teaching days by my principal, who told me she took the idea from a principal for whom she had once worked. No one knows where the Monday Memo came from. I am sure there are variations of it at most schools. If a campus has never used that tool and now they do long after you left, that's a part of your institutional legacy. So are Mrs. Little's conversion of the teacher's lounge to a computer lab or changing the school mascot, mission statement, or school colors. No one other than you may know how those things came to be and that you were the driver behind those decisions. That's your institutional legacy.

When you spend years or decades on a campus, it is inevitable that a part of you will remain. Your legacy is what you make it, from creating homecoming traditions to giving teachers a voice in campus decision-making. You usually don't get to say what your legacy will be, so make sure you leave enough fodder for the staff who remain to use afterward. Perhaps demanding lesson plans and yelling at students from the roof are my only legacy, but to me, they are depictions of my **Principal Presence** and **Principal Mystique**.

"The greatest legacy veteran principals can leave is to share their wealth of knowledge with the next generation of school leaders" (Bugbee, 2006).

The best measure of a principal's personal and institutional legacy is how many teachers and APs grew in their leadership to become teacher leaders, principals, and district leaders. It was almost a decade after leaving my last principalship that I realized my true legacy.

Wrapping up my annual session titled "Five Effective Systems for Every Principal" at the state principal association, some familiar faces came up to me. These were former teachers and APs of mine who went on to become principals. We hugged and reminisced about the good ol' days, and then they shared how they were trying to implement things I did.

- "OK, I know you might remember me complaining about lesson plans, but now I can't believe that none of my teachers have ever completed a lesson plan."

- "Gober, please, please, please explain more about your calendar setup. I am running around like a crazy person, and I can never get caught up."

- "You always made being a principal look so easy and fulfilling. It is why I wanted to be a principal."

- "I always thought you were just a severe case of Type A personality. I did not realize you actually had a master plan for what you did."

- "You need to write a manual or a book for me. I am dying, Gober, and I need help."

Perhaps this book is my legacy. I hope principals will use this book to become better principals. I want them to create the systems, structures, and schedules that allow less principal burnout and more improved schools to show that "Principals really matter."

Conclusion

As principals, we occupy a unique position of leadership that shapes not only the present but also the future of our schools, our staff, and our students. The systems and strategies discussed throughout this book serve as essential tools for cultivating a school environment that is both efficient and deeply connected. They are not just administrative tools. They are guiding principles for ensuring that every aspect of school leadership is intentional, impactful, and sustained over time.

A great principal is not merely a figurehead; they have a presence that is felt in every classroom, hallway, and conversation. This presence is amplified by consistency, transparency, and a clear vision that all stakeholders can see and support. But beyond this tangible presence is the *mystique*—the belief that the principal knows what is happening, cares deeply about it, and is involved in every success and challenge.

As you implement the five key systems outlined here, you'll see that leadership is not about sudden, sweeping changes but about persistent, well-monitored efforts that align with the needs and goals of your community. The ultimate goal is to leave behind a legacy of growth, improvement, and, most importantly, sustainability—one where, even in your absence, the systems you've put in place continue to thrive.

In closing, remember that **Principal Presence** and **Principal Mystique** are not strategies to be checked off a list; they embody the spirit of leadership that allows a school to succeed during your tenure and for many years to come. By mastering these approaches, you will improve the current state of your school and develop yourself as an effective instructional leader. You will also ensure a strong foundation for future leaders to build upon. And as you step away from your role one day, let your legacy reflect the time, care, and thoughtfulness you dedicated to making your school a beacon of excellence. Because, as we've seen time and again, *principals truly do matter*.

References

Attributed to Abraham Lincoln. *Note: This Quote Is Widely Attributed to Abraham Lincoln, Though Its Origin Is Uncertain.* n.c.

Attributed to Nelson Mandela. *Note: This Quote Is Widely Attributed to Nelson Mandela, Though Its Origin Is Uncertain.* n.d.

Attributed to Peter Drucker. *Note: This Quote Is Widely Attributed to Peter Drucker, Though Its Origin Is Uncertain.* n.d.

Bennis, Warren. *On Becoming a Leader.* New York: Basic Books, 2009.

Bryk, Anthony S., and Barbara Schneider. *Trust in Schools: A Core Resource for School Reform.* New York: Russell Sage Foundation, 2002.

Bugbee, Marjorie J. "The Greatest Legacy Veteran Principals Can Leave Is to Share Their Wealth of Knowledge with the Next Generation of School Leaders." *The Veteran Principal*, September/October 2006.

Cain, John, and Jim Laird. *The Fundamental Five: The Formulas for Quality Instruction.* Larchmont, NY: Eye on Education, 2011.

Collins, Jim. *Good to Great.* London: Random House Business Books, 2001.

Covey, Stephen R. *The 7 Habits of Highly Effective People: Powerful Lessons in Personal Change.* New York: Free Press, 1989.

DeWitt, Peter. "Todd Whitaker Already Said It." *Education Week*, September 27, 2012. https://www.edweek.org/education/opinion-todd-whitaker-already-said-it/2012/09.

DuFour, Richard, Rebecca DuFour, Robert Eaker, and Thomas Many. *Learning by Doing: A Handbook for Professional Learning Communities at Work.* Bloomington, IN: Solution Tree Press, 2006.

DuFour, Richard, Rebecca DuFour, Robert Eaker, and Thomas Many. *Learning by Doing: A Handbook for Professional Learning Communities at Work.* 3rd ed. Bloomington, IN: Solution Tree Press, 2016.

Edmonson, Amy. "Building a Psychologically Safe Workplace." *TEDx Talks*, September 2014. Video, 11:39. https://www.youtube.com/watch?v=LhoLuui9gX8.

Epstein, Joyce L. *School, Family, and Community Partnerships: Preparing Educators and Improving Schools.* Boulder, CO: Westview Press, 2001.

Fullan, Michael. *Leading in a Culture of Change.* San Francisco: Jossey-Bass, 2001.

Grissom, Jason A., Anna J. Egalite, and Constance A. Lindsay. *How Principals Affect Students and Schools: A Systematic Synthesis of Two Decades of Research.* New York: The Wallace Foundation, 2021. http://www.wallacefoundation.org/principalsynthesis.

Hallinger, Philip. "Leading Educational Change: Reflections on the Practice of Instructional and Transformational Leadership." *Cambridge Journal of Education* 33, no. 3 (2003): 329–51.

Harris, Alma, Christopher Day, David Hopkins, Mark Hadfield, Andy Hargreaves, and Christopher Chapman. *Effective Leadership for School Improvement.* London: Routledge Falmer, 2003.

International Baccalaureate. "Discover Why IB Students Succeed." August 20, 2024. https://www.ibo.org/university-admission/discover-why-ib-students-succeed/.

Koretz, Mark, and Mark Hollmann. *Urinetown: The Musical.* 2001.

Legal Digest. What Does the Paperwork Reduction Act Have to Do with Teacher Lesson Plans?" April 30, 2015. Retrieved from https://ed311.com/legal-digest-archive/what-does-the-paperwork-reduction-act-have-to-do-with-teacher-lesson-plans/.

Leithwood, Kenneth, Alma Harris, and David Hopkins. "Seven Strong Claims About Successful School Leadership." *School Leadership & Management* 28, no. 1 (2008): 27–42.

Leithwood, Kenneth, Karen Seashore, Stephen Anderson, and Kyla Wahlstrom. *Review of Research: How Leadership Influences Student Learning.* The Wallace Foundation, 2004. https://wallacefoundation.org/sites/default/files/2023-07/How-Leadership-Influences-Student-Learning.pdf.

Lemov, Doug. *Teach Like a Champion: 49 Techniques That Put Students on the Path to College.* San Francisco: Jossey-Bass, 2010.

Marzano, Robert J. *The New Art and Science of Teaching.* Bloomington, IN: Solution Tree Press, 2017.

Marzano, Robert J., Philip Warrick, and Julia A. Simms. *A Handbook for High Reliability Schools: The Next Step in School Reform.* Bloomington, IN: Marzano Research Laboratory, 2014.

Marzano, Robert J., Philip Warrick, Cameron Rains, and Richard DuFour. *Leading a High Reliability School.* Bloomington, IN: Solution Tree Press, 2018.

Marzano, Robert J., Timothy Waters, and Brian A. McNulty. *School Leadership That Works: From Research to Results.* Alexandria, VA: ASCD, 2005.

Merriam-Webster. Communication. In *Merriam-Webster.com Dictionary*, n.d. Retrieved from https://www.merriam-webster.com/dictionary/communication.

National Association of Secondary School Principals. "Extracurricular Participation and Academic Success." *Principal Leadership* 17, no. 4 (2016). https://www.nassp.org/publication/principal-leadership/volume-17-2016-2017/principal-leadership-december-2016/extracurricular-participation-and-academic-success/.

National Center for Education Statistics. *Extracurricular Participation and Student Engagement*. 1995. https://nces.ed.gov/pubs95/web/95741.asp.

OpenAI. "Communication Issues as a Root Cause for Problems." n.d. Retrieved July 2, 2024, from chatgpt.com.

Ordal, Todd. "CEO Coaching: The Unpredictable Leader." April 8, 2024. https://toddordal.com/ceo-coaching-the-unpredictable-leader/.

Owings, William A., and Leslie S. Kaplan. *Leadership and Organizational Behavior in Education: Theory into Practice*. Upper Saddle River, NJ: Pearson, 2013.

Pahl, Nadine, and Anne Richter. *SWOT Analysis: Idea, Methodology, and a Practical Approach*. Norderstedt: GRIN Verlag, 2009.

Sergiovanni, Thomas J. *Leadership for the Schoolhouse: How Is It Different? Why Is It Important?* San Francisco: Jossey-Bass, 1996.

Stevenson, Howard H., and Mihnea Moldoveanu. "The Power of Predictability." *Harvard Business Review* 73, no. 4 (1995): 140–9.

UCLA School Mental Health Project. n.d. https://smhp.psych.ucla.edu/.

Whitaker, Todd. *What Great Principals Do Differently: Eighteen Things That Matter Most*. 2nd ed. New York: Routledge, 2012.

Whitaker, Todd. *What Great Teachers Do Differently: Seventeen Things That Matter Most*. 2nd ed. Larchmont, NY: Eye On Education, 2012.

Wiggins, Grant, and Jay McTighe. *Understanding by Design*. Alexandria, VA: ASCD, 1998.

Wong, Harry K. *The First Days of School: How to Be an Effective Teacher*. Mountain View, CA: Harry K. Wong Publications, 2005.